I *Love* My Kids, But I Don't Always *Like* Them

Expert Advice For Parents of Challenging Children

Franki Bagdade, M. Ed.

*Academic and Behavioral Consultant,
Teacher, Coach, Blogger, and Mom*

For information, contact
MSI Press, LLC
1760-F Airline Hwy #203
Hollister, CA 95023

Editor: David Tabatsky
Copyeditor: Van Wolverton
Cover design: Carl Leaver
Cover photo: Lauren Giuliani
Inside photographs: Lauren Giuliani & Franki Bagdade
Layout: Opeyemi Ikuborije

LCCN: 9781950328956
ISBN: 9781950328895

To my dad for instilling the art of storytelling in me.

CONTENTS

Foreword

I *Love* My Kids, But I Don't Always *Like* Them

A Word from My Editor

As a parent, educator, and co-author of several parenting books, I laughed immediately at the title of Franki's book. Even more important, I related to her entire approach to managing the assorted challenges parents are facing today in what's becoming a rapidly ridiculous and demanding world. Obviously, this becomes more complicated and demanding when you consider children with special needs, whether they've been clinically diagnosed or not.

America is a society of "special" families, each with their own unique set of demands. Our diversity and differences define us, yet many parents whose children require "extra help" are not getting the assistance they need.

I Love My Kids, But I Don't Always Like Them! is filled with practical advice for approaching unavoidable dilemmas and invaluable lessons about the link between special needs and issues of self-esteem, depression, substance abuse and relationship failures, to name just a few of the risks involved with all kinds of kids as they grow up.

It speaks to millions of moms and dads and teachers and babysitters— all caring for children from pre-school to high school—who are struggling to figure out how to handle these remarkable and somewhat mystifying human creatures. They *love* them, for sure, but do they always *like* them?

This conundrum becomes exponentially magnified when a child does not meet conventional expectations, especially when it comes to age-appropriate milestones, such as achieving daily tasks, being socially interactive, focusing properly, managing school or establishing healthy relationships with his or her siblings.

Sound familiar? Is your family struggling because one of your children seems to consume all of your parental energy? Are you living with a "special" child? If so, then I Love *My Kids, But I Don't Always* Like *Them!* is for you.

Based on Franki's experience as a parent and her twenty-year career—as a teacher, resource consultant, and camp director—focusing primarily on children with behavioral challenges, she has guided many parents and educators on how to improve a child's behavior while empowering them to learn from and enjoy that child.

It should come as no surprise that this book is full of humorous moments, because as my family can attest—and Franki's, too—there may not be a better example of how to do things wrong than what the "expert" in the house aptly demonstrates.

Franki's sage advice is merely a result of listening well to those she encounters and using her professional experience to create a useful and inspiring book for those who need it most. While research shows that every family is different, there are a host of common denominators in raising "difficult" children successfully.

This book is short by design to make it accessible for its intended audience, who have limited time to read and need help dosed out in manageable bites. If you know families with special needs children, you know exactly what I mean.

I Love *My Kids, But I Don't Always* Like *Them!* provides an inspiring toolkit for these families in need. Its survival lessons will help parents and educators discover optimal solutions to the problems they are facing so that the children they care about will feel appreciated and loved—while the adults get some much-needed peace of mind.

—David Tabatsky

New York City

Acknowledgments

Thank you to my children, who know that I love them to pieces (I promise). I only don't like them every once in a while for a fleeting moment.

To my husband, Jeff, who quietly gets me and cheers me on.

To my mom, for spending countless hours around the kitchen table, helping me with homework, who knew that I would go from the child who could hardly write a five-paragraph essay to an author.

To my editor, David, for getting my sense of humor and helping me to give my manuscript the final shine it needed, while honoring my voice.

For my "Mom Tribe," you've taught me so much of what I know about motherhood and listened to me complain and kvell about it. You've taught me so much about who I wanted to be when I grew up as *we* grew up together.

To all of the bosses and mentors I've had along the way, who got *it* and got me, who were not concerned about me talking too much because they knew my passion, who didn't judge the pensive look on my face, because that was just me—growing and planning and thinking and discovering where the magic happens. Thanks, too, to the ones who didn't care if I was a little disorganized (or a lot disorganized) in ways that didn't actually matter.

And thank you to those along the way who didn't believe in me, get me, value me and honor me. You've made me more driven and steadfast in my goals and have given me the opportunity through shear desperation and necessity to really get to know myself again and to honor the fact that I love myself even if I don't always like myself.

Introduction

I *Love* My Kids, But I Don't Always *Like* Them

Introduction

The sound of your newborn baby crying for the first-time echoes in your brain forever. During the many months leading up to the birth, you dreamt of who that boy or girl would be, what they would look like and how it would feel when they became part of your family. Then suddenly, in a one moment frozen in time, that vision became real and alive, in the form of a helpless smush of a baby.

"I got this."

I was confident, and maybe even a little bit obnoxious, as a second-time mom. My almost two-year-old was on a tight sleep schedule, slept through the night consistently and was a pleasure. I told anyone who would listen, quite smugly I might add, that my first child gladly played by herself, while I happily scrolled through this new phenomenon called Facebook, answered emails, talked on the phone and read books. In fact, I often felt guilty complaining to my husband that I had too much time to myself, so I re-watched the original *90210* and joined a book club. I was living the mom dream!

I worked one day a week, doing educational testing for my former school, keeping myself current and in the loop. I was primarily a dedicated stay-at-home mom, and I was rocking it. I knew I was lucky to have a kid with a mild temperament, but I also thought I made it easy by reading all the right parenting books and following the advice. The idea of having another child, less than two years after we had our first, made perfect sense to me.

Flash forward 23 months—after we became parents for the second time. I was back in the hospital, flat on my back in the operating room, having my second C-section. In the most vulnerable of all positions, unable to see much at all, I heard that beautiful cry once again and watched the nurse hand this precious new baby to my husband.

"She looks just like your Uncle Rob," Jeff said.

This one was blond, round, and feisty—like me—and she was all mine. We affectionally referred to her as my Mini Me! Our oldest started preschool two mornings a week immediately after my husband's paternity leave ended, so I figured I'd still have plenty of time by myself to binge watch more shows. Of course, they would both nap, like clockwork, as I was an expert sleep trainer!

That first week, I invited a friend to hang out with Mini and me. It was just around that time when I began to notice something different about Kid #2. There was more crying than I remember. I figured I was just tired from waking up in the middle of the night, something I hadn't done for a year and a half, so I shrugged it off.

While my friend visited, Mini constantly cried. She was not wet or poopy or hungry or even particularly tired. I asked my friend what I was missing. For sure this was "fixable," and I just didn't know Gabi's different cries yet. My friend looked at me and smiled.

"You have a normal baby this time, Franki. This one will cry for no reason."

I shrugged her off since I had read all those excellent books. I mean, I had a master's degree in special education, for crying out loud, and I was adept at teaching children who had been kicked out of their home schools for misbehavior. I certainly wasn't going to let a baby intimidate me, and definitely not my own!

However, I also knew my friend was right because Gabi *did* cry all the time, and for no reason! This was maddening and exhausting. I felt like a complete failure. I understood why my friends always exchanged weird looks as my oldest child, Ruby, sat happily in a high-chair, an Exersaucer or a stroller—for hours...as if she were born to chill. Maybe that was luck and not my parenting skills. Maybe that wasn't normal?!?

Slowly, I started to see that things were different this time. My husband still recalls, with a look of fear in his eyes, how he used to get home from work, park his car in the driveway, and hear shrieking inside the house. He would have a moment each day, thankfully only a moment, when he wasn't sure if he should get out of the car and set foot inside our home.

Prompted by Gabi's incessant crying, I became obsessed with charting, tracking, and watching how she behaved. From my many years working with tough kids who could not control their emotions, I knew there had to be a reason behind her behavior, even as an infant. Once I was open to discovering these reasons and got over my anger at having such a cranky baby, I learned quite a few things about this smushy meatloaf of a human being.

Gabi became overstimulated really easily, and the only thing that could bring her back to zero was sleep. So, she took many naps. Not little cute naps in my arms, a stroller or a bouncy seat, like other babies. Friends kept trying to reassure me that babies this age didn't need a nap schedule and they could just sleep anywhere.

I guess Gabi wasn't briefed on this expectation, because that never happened for us! My daughter needed total silence and darkness in a crib. Thankfully, many of my friends had kids and a spare crib or two to lend us. While we visited and socialized, she managed to sleep all over town in other people's cribs—never for long, but those short bursts of sleep erased whatever had over-stimulated her in the first place. Once she had her "baby power" nap, she would eat or play and appear to be quite content.

The smiles were there—I know because I have pictures to prove it— but when I close my eyes and remember that time and that baby, I see a straight-faced, no-party-tricks child. I remember watching little old ladies cooing at her in the shopping cart and their look of confusion as a blank-faced baby stared right back at them, unwilling to smile or budge.

I always had the feeling that my daughter had no interest in being a baby, certainly not an adorable one for strangers, and detested the lack of control that came with being temporarily stuck in that age and maybe in diapers, too. "I am not here to be cute for you!"

She made up for this frustration by crawling and walking early and gaining independence much faster than her people-pleasing delight of an older sister. When my friends complained about their babies and toddlers getting into everything as they became mobile, I was finally able to relax. Being "normal" felt like a welcome exception.

That little piece of heaven didn't last long. My energetic Mini Me only liked me. This was not ideal when I desperately wanted help from my husband, a grandparent or a babysitter. However, this worked out perfectly when it was just the two of us, as we delightfully walked through the aisles of grocery stores, content with each other's company. She would never run away from me and was so happy to walk on her own two feet. Thank God for small favors.

In fact, the "Terrible Twos" never arrived, and Gabi was a much easier toddler than a baby. Of course, this pattern developed while my formerly easy first child started to have some new needs of her own, and almost overnight I was forced to become a champion juggler of multiple childhood concerns. This happened more and more, day after day, until I felt as though I was juggling fire, on a unicycle, blindfolded, with one hand tied behind my back.

As Mini Me turned three, her crying became what I called "raging," consistent, loud and brutal. At first, I thought it came out of nowhere. I now know that this is not true because there is always a pattern, and behavior is always communication, as my behavior modification philosophy has proven, though it took me several missteps to figure out what these tantrums were all about. At the time, though, her behavior felt nonsensical, unpredictable, and for sure, unnecessary. My collection of parenting books was no help, either.

I couldn't reason my little independent (adult) three-year-old out of this pattern. After trying a few million assorted strategies (or maybe it just felt like that), including some I would never recommend, such as yelling, bribing, and making a show of crying myself, I decided to embark on a different approach. I chose to just let it happen, deliberately, but I refused to engage or become be part of her "stuff."

I trained myself to calmly pick her up, hold her steady, look at her in the eyes and speak in a calm and even tone. "I see you're crying, and you're hurting my ears. Sit here (on this step, couch, cereal aisle, floor, etc.) until you're totally calmed down and then I can help you."

This technique worked miraculously. My friends stood back in horror and relief that their kids didn't require this kind of response, but they were in awe of how it worked—every time. They were in awe, and I was relieved at a level I never knew existed.

One time, I was in a large grocery store when Gabi started melting down in the checkout line about candy or something. I gently put her on the floor next to me and totally ignored her crying. Let's be real. She was screaming. Loudly. There's no such thing as mellow screaming. I somehow heard the cashier and talked over my daughter's imitation of a horror movie during the whole transaction. Eventually, due to some unknown miracle, my daughter's rage turned into silent sniffles. The cashier looked back and forth between me and my sniffling child. Then she said one of the most significant things I've ever heard during my mommying career.

"Ma'am, I see a lot of parenting going on in this store," she said, "and that was the best I've ever encountered." I will forever be grateful for her validation, which was more important to me than she will ever know. That single sentence clicked right away and told me I was on to something. Soon after that encounter, I started to realize that my combination of life experiences actually added up to something, and that maybe what I found to work effectively with Gabi could help other parents or teachers.

From then on, I actually looked forward to going grocery shopping.

My inclination to help other parents came from being a child growing up with ADHD and anxiety; my training as an educator and then a special education teacher and consultant; my experience in the classroom with children who have special needs; my consulting work supporting frustrated teachers, and then moving into the world of summer camps, when the behavior was all about social skills and independence.

Taken all together, along with my own recent parenting challenges, I knew I was on the right track and that I wanted to help other families feel less helpless. I wanted all moms and dads out there to know that it was okay to struggle. I wanted them to know that you can *love* your child fiercely and not *like* them so much all the time.

Don't worry, I never play favorites among my own children (or yours), and I feel this way from time to time about all three of mine! (Maybe don't tell them, though, thank you.)

The fact that you are wondering right now if you are doing this parenting thing "right" and the fact that you picked up this book or any book to try and parent better, means that you are already a great parent. Things can get better, though, and more consistent and even predictable, and you can learn to enjoy living with your tough one. I want to help.

Let's begin with how to read this book. Each chapter describes the steps I use and the questions I ask myself daily as a mom, as a consultant, educator, and frankly, as a human being, when I encounter difficult behavior. This helps me to genuinely enjoy people. It helps me to enjoy my kids more, too, but not always, and that's okay! Remember, you are not a monster if you think your supposedly adorable baby is not so adorable. That applies to toddlers, too, and the beat goes on.

Each chapter focuses on a different topic, weaved together with our stories—told as creative fiction, or fables, if you will, inspired by cold hard facts. Each story is based on my history as a teacher, consultant, camp director, mom and more. In order to protect the privacy of my students, clients and my own kids, each child and parent is a combo of those I have worked with throughout my 20+ year career.

What if you need help now? What if you are liking your kid very little these days? First of all, it's okay to feel that way. You are not a bad person, and you are not alone! It can get better. I recommend reading chapters one and six right away and then you can pick and choose the other ones according to which ones are a good fit for your particular parenting dilemma(s).

Don't forget: if you are questioning if you are a good mom or dad... you are!

1

Right Size Your Expectations!

As your new reality sinks in,

you start to have flashbacks

of sitting at the kitchen table with
your mother,

arguing over homework and requesting

your favorite foods for dinner.

As you revisit those old tapes,

you realize that this is your life now.

You're the one in charge of scheduling

and menus and rules of behavior.

Right Size Your Expectations!

One day, you open your eyes and realize you've been sleeping on a regular basis, as if you're a real human being! Most nights, those evolving little humans you created now fall asleep without any complicated strategy and they wake up feeling refreshed. You no longer keep a running tab of how many hours in a row you actually slept or even how many nights your children didn't wake you up at three a.m. to eat a peach or discuss their favorite cartoon. Free of these chronic disturbances, you and your spouse don't argue about who has woken up more before dawn (spoiler alert, I won that fight), and that realization is life changing. If you're not there yet, you will be one day, I promise. It happens to the weariest of us.

With the renewed confidence this sleep will bring, not to mention what it can do for your health, you may start leaving the baby gates open or take them down all together. You might even put the diaper genie out with the trash with a tear of happiness in your eye. Whatever ritual it may be, it is now residing in your rearview mirror.

You can finally relax. Hallelujah!

Believe it or not, you can make dinner without holding a child in one arm. I'm not saying you *want* to make dinner, but technically you could... or should. You begin saving thousands of dollars on diapers and baby food. You beam with pride as your child navigates Netflix independently, at least until he or she discovers a movie that you might not even be brave enough to watch. You can leave the room without worrying about the sharp edges of your coffee table causing your child to have a near death experience. You might go as far as removing the giant emergency number magnets from your refrigerator and stashing them in a nearby drawer... just in case.

Then, your adorable child returns home from a day in kindergarten with a backpack bigger than she is and shows you her daily planner, reading log, homework folder, PTO flyer packet, spirit week dress-up list, and instructions for a Google log in. In that moment, your heart sinks a bit.

Hmm, now what? Do I have a guidebook for what happens next?

The baby center doesn't offer a forum on what to do with your kid now that she is beginning to have a life of her own. I check YouTube but can't find an appropriate training video for this juncture in my parenting life. I thought they had one for *everything* under the sun. I planned for life with babies and toddlers and took pride in continually being able to outrun them, but I'm not sure I was prepared for kids!

As your new reality sinks in, you start to have flashbacks of sitting at the kitchen table with your mother, arguing over homework and requesting your favorite foods for dinner. As you revisit those old tapes, you realize that this is *your* life now. You're the one in charge of scheduling and menus and rules of behavior. In a moment of great remorse, you call your parents and beg for forgiveness for being such a giant pain in the ... they know what.

You can't escape and take a nap. Oh no, that's not allowed or even advised. You're on your own because your spouse has cleverly figured out how to be employed and spend eight to ten hours a day in an alternate location. You are being left to your own devices and I don't mean your phone or laptop.

Why didn't anyone write *What to Expect Five Years After You're Expecting?*

You need the sequel right now, a step-by-step guide to parenting through these basics. It's hard to comprehend how people do this every day, seven days a week, for years! You are drowning in lunchboxes and homework and flyers and the paperwork that comes along with modern child rearing. You think you have mastered the color-coded Google calendars, yet you and your daughter still manage to show up for other kids' birthday parties on the wrong day and pediatrician appointments in the wrong week (not that I have any firsthand experience with this.)

Just when you think you can't take one more interruption or surprise or disturbance, as in "Mommy, I have to tell you about this *thing*," your child may bring up a whole new set of issues you never anticipated while you were playing peek-a-boo, changing diapers and blowing bubbles. Almost overnight, you start hearing your child complain and question kids at school who are not being kind. She wonders aloud whose birthday parties she is being invited to and who is not including her. She doesn't understand why her soccer coach didn't let her score all the goals, not realizing yet that she's playing on a team instead of in her own backyard.

The issues can be anything. Some kids struggle to read; some struggle to sit still; some don't understand why they can't make friends, and some teach themselves how to read and find school instruction a bore.

You have parent/teacher conferences and see bar graphs comparing your child's skills to those in their district and across the country. You hold your breath, hoping that your child's teacher "gets them" because they are so much more than their test scores, lunch account number, virtual passwords, and cubby #4. Do they see what you see? Don't they realize that your son or daughter truly *is* the cat's meow, even if they are actually allergic to cats, and peanuts and eggs?

This perfectly imperfect human being, who makes your heart explode with joy and your extremities tremble in fear and confusion at every turn, is now becoming an actual person. And then, for no apparent reason, seemingly out of the blue, you're not sleeping again. The kids are sleeping, but you are not. Your spouse? Let's not go there. (How do they do it?)

Who thought I could do this, anyway?

Parenting? Actual little people?

I mean seriously, how do I know when to worry and when it's a phase?

I took a birthing and baby safety course when I was pregnant, but no one trained me for raising actual children! How do I know what is normal? When does my worrying become productive and necessary? When is the stress I feel a result of good parenting? When is all the fretting just wasted time and energy?

I've looked everywhere and no one has come up with a cute name for "The Driving Me Crazy Sixes." I can't find any help when I Google "The Sassy McSassy Eights." No one has anything to say about "The Old Enough for Boarding School Tens." The internet goes nowhere with "The She Knows Everything and Could Parent Better Than Me Twelves."

After more than 20 years sitting on the other side of the table with parents, and from learning from my own mistakes, here is my advice to other parents: *Listen to the experts, even when it hurts.* Listen to teachers, pediatricians, and camp directors. If a professional working with your child has a concern and shares it with you, just thank them and listen.

Let me repeat. Listen.

Whatever is going on may be no cause for concern; however, these professionals observe countless adolescents on any given day and know when a child stands out for reasons that require compassionate attention. If your situation needs legit consultation, why wait until it gets out of hand? What's the point in that? No one is keeping score. There won't be a neighborhood billboard going up to announce that you're not a perfect parent. After all, that would require a perfect parent to put it up and they don't exist!

So, if you think you need help, ask for it! If you are struggling with parenting, which we *all* do, then this is a good time to check your defensiveness at the door! Listen to yourself as well. If your parent intuition tells you something isn't quite right, and if you observe major differences in your child and others of a similar age, it's time to consult an expert.

You can always start with your pediatrician or your child's teacher or social worker. If your child needs additional help, they can probably guide you to the right place and person. (You will find professional consultants, etc. in the Resources section in the back of the book.)

Before you settle in for another sleepless night, study up on your child's age and know what to expect and what not to expect. This will give you some perspective and maybe even comfort as you go forward to try and solve the issue.

In my experience as a teacher consultant, I am often brought into a classroom for a specific concern and realize that the child in question is showing developmentally appropriate learning or social skills. Checking their record, I see that they just happen to be the youngest in their class and a little behind on the developmental curve. This is especially true if you are in an affluent community where parents are well-educated and able to offer language rich environments for their children.

It's also important to remember that young children, from birth to age seven, change and grow quite rapidly. "I blinked, and my son went from diapers to winning chess tournaments!"

All joking aside, if you're comparing your child to someone just a few months older, you may not be evaluating their development appropriately. If you're not sure, seek out a reputable resource, such as your local, county or state health department. Examine ages and stages, and ask your pediatrician for more information or consult reputable sources online, like The Centers for Disease Control (CDC) or The American Academy of Pediatrics, which just brush the surface of what is available nationally or in your specific area.

Once you better understand what is developmentally expected of your child, you can get to know your children as the awesome individuals they are. Respect their personal limits by adjusting your expectations because one size does not fill all, not even close.

By keeping an open mind and embracing good advice, you can learn to enjoy your child again. What a gift that would be for both of you. To be honest, you won't be blissfully parenting all the time, and it would be foolish to expect that, but that's okay; it's normal. This is a hard job, but someone's got to do it!

You love your children, but you don't always like them. Sound familiar? Join the club.

Expectations in the Bagdade Family

My kids need sleep! All kids do, of course, but mine take it to the next level. This was awesome when they were little because most evenings, after they were all tucked in, I could enjoy alone time with my husband. I might be going out on a limb here, but I think he'll agree. (Or completely ignore my husband and watch the newest romantic comedy alone!)

Now, our oldest still needs more sleep than the younger two. She could probably win an Olympic sleeping competition. This proficiency made her the world's best baby! It's become a little trickier as she gets older and wants to stay out late and have a social life. It's especially tricky when she wants to stay up extra late to watch *Vampire Diaries* because that usually means that the next day (and maybe the one after that, too) we all have to deal with her dedicated crankiness or moodiness or whichever -ness you want to call it.

In the spirit of full disclosure, let me tell you something right here and now. If you think that whining and meltdowns will end by the time your child becomes a teenager, then I have news for you—and a teen to lend you for the weekend! Adolescence, which is a polite way to put it, is a challenge to any parent's sanity. Of course, life happens, and we want our "maturing" children to be able to experience special occasions, such as trips, live theater, family celebrations and extra movie nights, just to name a few from the demand list.

Some kids are super flexible in this regard and that is completely normal and most welcome. However, mine are not, and this is also completely normal, and not most welcome. To explain, my kids just don't have fun after a certain time. I know better than to expect age-appropriate behavior from my seven-year-old after nine p.m. If I did, this would be setting myself up for real disappointment, not to mention a headache, and whoever is with us at any given time—grandparents, friends or strangers looking on in horror—will be subjected to behavior that, let's just say, they'd rather not witness.

Sometimes, the novelty of an exciting activity will stretch him a little longer into the evening, and when this happens, some extra sugar doesn't hurt. (How old do they have to be before having a Coke? Asking for a friend.) On any given night, he may regress and become a cranky preschooler as we hit his "being awake too long wall" and that's okay. It's up to me, as the expert on my little guy, to expect this, to plan accordingly, and sometimes say no to late activities. (Yes, you *can* say no!)

When he's lying on the floor with his eyes closed at 9:15 p.m., smack in the middle of my cousin's Bar Mitzvah party (true story), and family members are wandering by, wondering why I'm not "fixing" this problem, it's really my fault for having him awake this late.

He's not misbehaving! It's not his fault at all. So, he cannot be blamed at all either. Realistic expectations on my part should have prepared me for this exact moment, and I must be confident in the fact that it's natural and following his usual pattern and it's now my problem and not his. Believe me, I will pay the price for the next two or three days, as my normally happy-go-lucky seven-year-old acts more like the world's whiniest three-year-old.

This is not a behavioral issue that needs "fixing." No bribe, behavior chart or clear expectations will likely change his behavior. In this case, I'm the one who must "right size" my expectations and share the burden of doing whatever is needed to help him restore his normal equilibrium. This doesn't mean that we never keep our little guy out past his bedtime; we just pick and choose what situations will not compromise our exceptions in the wrong way, which means that sometimes when we may leave him home with a babysitter.

My middle child, however, has boundless energy, and since she was nine, she has been handling an 8:30 p.m. end-time for her midweek dance classes. In fact, she sleeps much better on dance nights!

My oldest child hates running errands. To her, going to the grocery store represents a special type of medieval torture, comparable to a despicable, impossible world with no iPhones or TikTok. No! Not that, please! Considering her limited capacity to shop for food, I pick my battles. She's now old enough to stay home alone, and I will go out of my way to drop her off at home when time allows.

When she was little, this conundrum meant less errand productivity during the week for me and more on the weekend, when my husband was home. It also meant that I was never going to be the mom who shopped at three grocery stores, determined to find the perfect watermelon, and I was going to have to adapt to finding everything as best as I could in one short stop, standing in one (hopefully) short line, similar to my favorite game show of the 90's, called "Super Market Sweep." This is way more pleasant for both of us. We may not end up with every cereal and snack on the shopping list, but we manage.

Of course, sometimes time doesn't allow for the luxury of her languishing at home while I do all the heavy lifting, and it becomes her turn to be flexible. In that case, it is appropriate to ask a 12-year-old to come along, but for my daughter this is only realistic some of the time. On those occasions, I prepare her for the disappointment, pretend I am wearing earplugs and ignore her grumbling. I don't expect her to turn into a combat soldier and become irrationally obedient. "Yes ma'am" is not an expected response—ever.

I often steal language from Jim Fay, the famous creator of the brilliant *Love and Logic*™ and try my luck with his approach. "Did I give you a choice yesterday about leaving the house? Did you get a choice at breakfast and again at lunch? Do you notice how many choices I've given you? You do? Great! Now it's my turn to make a choice, and I choose to stop at the grocery store. Thank you for cooperating!"

Once again, realistic expectations set us up for way less disappointment and kept our parenting portfolio from blowing up! If you happen to have a teen or tween, I don't recommend looking in the rearview mirror to catch the eye rolling after a Jim Fay decree like this one.

Some of you might be thinking that the world doesn't work this way, that kids have to get used to sucking it up, like adults do. Well, first of all, they are not adults. Let's pause right here and digest that as a fact. Calling a 15-year-old a young man or a young woman does not mean they are an adult! The 'man' and 'woman' part is also misleading and can definitely screw up our expectations, not to mention your kids, who usually want to grow up at the speed of sound, which might explain why they can be so noisy.

Teens and tweens should enjoy some extra flexibility until they are actually capable of making rational and reasonable decisions. Remember right sizing your expectations? This is absolutely necessary and can save your entire family a lot of grief … and ibuprofen … and other unmentionable treatments for advanced exasperation.

I expect some whining when I take my teen to the store with me, but not as much as when I bring my husband along (we are still working on this, but that's another book.)

Full disclosure: I actually hate grocery shopping! So, you know what I do? I pay $120 a year to Instacart and now I have most of my groceries delivered. Does that mean that I never learned "to just suck it up?" Nope! I still do what's necessary to have ample groceries in our house. At the same time, I accommodate myself and my own needs. (Imagine that? My own needs!) Along the way, I right sized the expectations I had put on myself! I still do plenty of daily tasks that I don't enjoy at all but are considered essential. It's just that grocery shopping (in person) surely isn't one of them.

Carma's Story

Every family has to figure out the expectation game and how each child may respond to surprises, frustration, disappointment and even too much excitement. As children grow up, and their behavior evolves, their capacity to handle change and respond to unwelcome triggers may also vary, depending on a number of factors. Every family must deal with this process.

The Greens came to me because their daughter kept embarrassing them at family functions. Both parents had four siblings, and everyone lived nearby, so they came together to enjoy a meal at least once a week. Carma's parents considered this a blessing, but their daughter wasn't so appreciative. As she turned 12, she often tried to get out of family events by crying and begging to stay home alone.

I facilitated a parent-child meeting with them (see Chapter 6). After some open-ended questions, Carma was able to verbalize that she felt nervous being with large groups of people, especially among her aunts and uncles. While well-meaning and loving, they couldn't stop launching tons of nonstop questions toward Carma, which made her anxious.

After speaking with Carma and her parents and teachers, I suspected that she had difficulty processing auditory language quickly. This made all the questioning from well-intentioned family feel like a rapid-fire assault. With so much background noise at these large family functions, she may not have been able to hear the questions being directed at her and would struggle to comprehend them and process her thoughts into an age-appropriate answer. To compensate, she would often answer, "I don't know" to even simple questions, such as "How's soccer going this season?" This frustrated Carma's family, especially her grandparents, who thought she was being rude.

Children with invisible disabilities, such as language disorders, ADHD, and anxiety often appear rude when they are actually trying their best! I suggested to Carma's parents that they work with their school district to get Carma a full Speech and Language Evaluation (more about how to get your child expert support in the Resources section.)

As I expected, Carma had a speech and language disability. She was severely delayed in receptive language, which refers to processing language as it comes in. No wonder she could not quickly come up with sufficient answers to all the small talk!

According to the K-12 Teachers Alliance,Top of Form while learning disabilities are common, many myths are attached to them, which can be detrimental to how these students socialize and are educated. When children have a disability, their parents must navigate new territory. As educators, it's our responsibility to demystify these disabilities. So, when it came to Carma's mom and dad, I assured them from the start that her issues were absolutely not a result of harmful or neglectful parenting.

Carma and her parents became educated about her language disability, and she received some great speech and language therapy to address it. However, she remained anxious about going to family functions. She was not quite ready to share her diagnosis with her huge extended family and asked her parents to keep it private. She wanted to enjoy these gatherings like her siblings and cousins and was just as frustrated as her parents with her lack of ability to do so. She wasn't misbehaving when she had meltdowns before going to those family dinners; she was simply communicating her fear and anxiety in the only way she could.

Eventually, with the new language skills she acquired, Carma was able to have more comfortable conversations, but she still became fatigued and "talked out" more quickly than your average 12-year-old and she didn't want to continue disappointing everyone. Her parents wanted to "right size" their expectations as they supported their daughter to demonstrate age-appropriate behavior by not letting her anxiety get in her own way.

Carma's Family Dinner Plan

Here is the plan we came up with, collaboratively and preventatively, for the Green's next Sunday night family dinner, which was hosted at Carma's aunt's house. It was typically quite noisy, and most of the adults were asking many questions, which was expected. Carma's parents even reminded her of this.

Here's what we decided we could control: The Green family will be the first of the extended family to arrive. When they are the only ones joining the hosts, the atmosphere is calm, warm, and inviting and that becomes Carma's first impression. She can enjoy playing with her cousins with no competition for their attention and catch up with her aunt and uncle when it's just two families interacting.

Beginning the evening this way lessoned Carma's anxiety. The Greens and I clearly explained to her what was appropriate and expected for someone her age in this situation. We even modeled some back-and-forth conversation skills she could use when talking to adults by deliberately "right sizing" our expectations to include Carma's language deficits. She could have one 10-minute break away from people and three short breaks of two to five minutes, but most of her time she should be with the family.

To help her take breaks without being asked why she was leaving the room, she brought a school novel and said she was doing homework. School is prioritized in her family and her parents thought that no one would interrupt her if she said she was doing homework. They asked ahead of time if she was able to use her aunt's office to get a little work done so she didn't fall behind, and her aunt happily complied.

Carma was a bit nervous that evening as they prepared to go for dinner, but her parents saw her confidence building as she now knew how to please them and her extended family! They reported that the night went beautifully. Carma focused on enjoying her little cousins, as we thought this would help her avoid the parts that were not ideal for her limitations. On the way home in the car, her parents, as instructed, immediately and specifically praised her behavior and accomplishments. Carma seemed proud of herself and expressed how much she enjoyed the experience and was even looking forward to the next family dinner!

Preparing for Trips

Whether it's a family dinner, a night out to the movies or a trip out of town, behavior can become a problem if expectations are not discussed beforehand.

When our family goes on a trip, I take time before we leave to explain to our children that there will be waiting, like in airports, while we're driving, or because of big-city traffic, and some of it will be excessive and annoying. I describe what the food will be like, how our days will be structured, sleeping arrangements, etc. Some of these explanations occur during a family meeting and some are communicated during one-on-one time. That way, I can customize how I manage some of the expectations according to the individual quirks of each kid, and believe me, they have quirks!

For my little ones, who were too young to remember their previous flight experiences, we went through every detail—what security would be like, where there would probably be long lines and when there would be lots of walking. We talked about car rides and how everyone was going to try to use the potty at every stop even if they didn't have to. You can have fun with it, and even practice at home by setting up chairs to look like you are on an airplane or pretend to go through security.

About a week before any of these trips, we go over the basic day-to-day schedule. As my kids have gotten older and I have learned more about their unique needs, this preparation hasn't always been done with the whole family. For example, my more anxious middle child sometimes needed this information at least a week in advance. Conversely, when we planned a trip out of the country, which made her extra anxious (she didn't like the idea of flying over the ocean) she asked not to talk about it until it was closer, and I obliged. My youngest loves traveling the most and wants to talk about it incessantly, which can really trigger his sister's anxiety to a high level, so we have taught him that we will talk about our upcoming travels only before bed when we can do it with just him on a one-to-one basis.

I'm also careful to let the kids know clearly what will *not* be happening.

For example, a few years after an eye-opening experience with our family Disney World trip (shared in the next chapter), we went back to Orlando. We only had Legoland on our itinerary. I knew we'd drive past the iconic Walt Disney World signs, so I made sure the kids knew that there wasn't a surprise trip in the cards. This was really important because a few years earlier we had surprised them with a day at Disneyland so that assumption on their part would make sense!

See? I really put myself in their brains when I'm planning a trip! It's much easier to let them be disappointed now, in the comfort of their own home, where they have the freedom to slam their own doors and tell us in private that we are the meanest parents ever!

Beyond explaining my behavioral expectations to all of my kids, I must consider their individual needs. My sensory-sensitive kiddo always has a literal and figurative toolbox with her. We call it her sensory backpack, complete with ear plugs, headphones, fidgets, and more. (Learn how to create your own in Chapter 3 or visit my YouTube channel, where Gabi explains her method!).

With prompts and suggestions from me, she decides what goes in it for each outing. My Olympic caliber, sleep-craving oldest child gets her own bed on these trips as much as possible, whenever we can swing it. My little guy gets to go to sleep as close to his bedtime as we can manage. This philosophy, which we put into action for big events and trips, also works well for other occasions, such as extended family events and one-day outings.

Key Points for Busy Moms and Dads

1. Understand what should be expected developmentally by utilizing available resources, such as your pediatrician and teachers, along with national organizations like the American Psychological Association and the Centers for Disease Control. (See the Resources section)

2. Don't compare your child to your friend's child. Don't even compare them to their brother or sister. They are one-of-a-kind, each and every one of them.

3. Know that all children, and adults for that matter, have strengths and weaknesses.

4. Watch out for behavioral patterns. If this observation could help Carma with her particular needs, then something similar might help other kids, too.

5. Plan ahead with your child. You're not only managing their expectations; you're handling yours, too. Planning ahead will do everyone a favor.

2

Taming Tantrums
after Toddlerhood

Tantrums, meltdowns, freak-outs
and fits—

no matter what you call them, they are
disruptive.

They can make us fear our children,

embarrass us in public

and cause us to lose our cool.

Taming Tantrums
after Toddlerhood

Welcome to the story of "Ikea Ruby." One quiet Sunday afternoon, my husband and I decided to take the kids to browse at IKEA, the first superstore of its kind in our area. That was our first mistake. Little did I know that IKEA resembles a casino, albeit with better lighting and no booze, but once you're inside more than a few minutes you lose all sense of time. Perhaps this is because the store has no windows and no easy way out.

It's a winding maze of a rabbit hole with an endless collection of colorful toys to beg for and my children were no different than any others when it comes to resisting cool stuff.

There was a blur, beginning with an irrational screaming child and a quick and desperate purchase of a stuffed animal, called *Barnslad Flaudhaus*. We're still not sure if it's a hippo or a yak.

IKEA hosted Ruby's worst ever tantrum. She was well over her toddler years by then, so it was alarming, to say the least. I can't tell you today what it was about or how we navigated through it. I can tell you how embarrassing it was and how terrifying and long-lasting the effects have been. To this day, any time she starts to get mad (even as a teen) my husband will whisper to me, "Uh oh, here comes Ikea Ruby!"

To be clear, I don't blame this on IKEA, but I do recommend that you think twice before venturing into stores this big and calculating with your children, especially if they are easily triggered by too much stimulation.

It's never good when a child has a tantrum within a hundred yards of a cash register.

My Secret Weapons

Tantrums, meltdowns, freak outs and fits—no matter what you call them, they are disruptive. They can make us fear our children, embarrass us in public and cause us to lose our cool! Just when you feel like you have made it through the *Terrible Twos* or the *Trying Threes*, disruptive forces rear their ugly head again and you find yourself Googling the *Satanic Sevens*.

Older kids, teens and even moms still have these behavioral hiccups, yet we tend to call them by other names, such as meltdowns or crack-ups or freak-outs, and we often hear people say things like, "She's losing it again" or "Watch out, the Exorcist is coming." Some of us are lucky enough to have more sensitive, high-needs kids who have these mood swings more frequently than we expect at their age.

Through my work with kids in the classroom, at camp and in my domestic life (at home, in the grocery store, at Grandma's house, in restaurants, at their sibling's choir concert, in the car or at the dealership), I have devised a little cheat sheet of ideas that have become my go-to secret weapon for these moments. By following the six tools included here, you will prevent many meltdowns. However, even with the best planning, they will still happen.

1. Validate

Level out your voice and remove your child from the equation. For example: "I'm so sorry that the rain is too dry for you. Your crying is hurting my ears. Please sit on this step (spot, bed, room, corner, couch) until you are all done crying and then we can talk about it."

With younger kids, you can pick them up and place them there, repeatedly if necessary. You can create a spot, called a calm down spot or cool down corner, or just a place somewhere where they can take a moment alone to be calm.

I am not calling it a time out or making it punitive. Your kids are not in trouble; they just may need a moment to get back to a place where they can communicate their needs. With an older child I will calmly say, "When your voice is calm, not screaming or crying, I'd love to talk with you." Later, when they are calm, you can have a parent/child meeting to determine the problem and come up with a plan (Chapter 6).

Evening out your voice is important, and hard to do at first. Take a deep breath and keep trying. If you yell or raise your voice, that could easily be perceived as negative attention, which may encourage more of the same behavior.

You also don't want to sound totally pleased with the meltdown. Keep your voice flat and even. With lots of practice, this will come naturally, most of the time, because parents have meltdowns, too. It's okay!

For young kids: "You seem upset, would you like a hug? (Give a hug only if they are not kicking or hitting.) When your voice is calm again, we can talk about what's bothering you."

For older kids: "I get it. You don't want to do your homework. In our house, we turn all our homework in on time. When you've stopped screaming and whining, I'm happy to help you. Let me know when you are ready."

For teens: "I'm sorry you are so disappointed with my decision about Saturday night. Dad and I made the choice that we feel is most appropriate for your age. We're happy to explain our reasoning to you, but not when you're yelling. Let us know when you're ready to have a calm, grown-up conversation. That would be great."

2. Ignore, Ignore, and Keep Ignoring

Harness your inner Hermione Granger and put your 'invisibility cloak' on and go about your business. Only talk to your child again when the screaming turns to sniffles. This is a great strategy for a kid who will not stay in their room, on a designated chair or in a calming spot. It's for the kid who just follows you around, no matter what. If you do use some words, keep them consistent and short.

You've validated first, offered a hug and so on. You are going to use this tool when the tantrum or meltdown has escalated, your kids need space and time for themselves, and you have nothing nice to say or you need space and time to deescalate.

3. Broken Record

When I taught this to camp counselors and young teaching assistants, they did not know what I meant by this, which made me feel quite old. Hopefully, you all do!

Repeat with no emotion:

"I'll talk to you when you are calm. I'll talk to you when you are calm. I'll talk to you when you are calm."

Don't mix it up and don't raise your voice.

Don't engage in a power struggle.

At first, a child's tantrum may get louder or bigger, as they become angry that you're not giving them what they want in the moment. Eventually, they realize that you mean business and they'll work to calm themselves.

4. Distract

Start with one of these lines to establish a solid baseline:

"Are those new shoes you're wearing?"

"Remind me, how many states are in the USA again? Which ones were original colonies?"

"Tell me that funny story again about your new puppy!"

This works beautifully with toddlers, but with older kids, too. Remember, in the middle of a tantrum you are not going to have a parent/child meeting or solve any issues. Your focus should only be on helping your child get back into a calm state.

A *screen time* distraction often works well here. You can give it a time limit of course but it *is* a nice distraction. You may be thinking, "What if my child is having a tantrum about being done with screen time?" In that case, I would not use that technique and you will need to do some big time ignoring.

Later, when the time is right, I would suggest having a screen time parent/child meeting to prevent this behavior next time the screen time has ended.

Being playful can be a distraction within itself.

"I know you don't want hamburgers for dinner. You need to try a few bites and you can have some pasta and carrots on the side. I know that's not what you want. Sometimes, I wish we could have ice cream sundaes for dinner, and you know what? I want them for lunch and breakfast, too. Oh, but then my stomach would hurt really bad from all of that ice cream. I'm going to try putting my hamburger on a bun with ketchup. Do you want to do that, too?"

5. Choices

Give your child two choices, both of which are acceptable to you. This gives them some control and still gets the job done.

"I know you don't want to shower today, Buddy, but you need to. Would you like to shower now or in 15 minutes?"

Follow this with a timer so they know when it is time to comply if they chose the delay!

"I know you don't want to participate in chores. However, in our family we're all part of keeping our house clean and we earn privileges this way. Would you like to continue with last week's chores or pick a new task for this week? Would you like to do a little of your bigger jobs every day or spend a big chunk of time on them over the weekend?"

Or "I know you don't want to do your homework; however, it's due tomorrow. Would you like to do it after dinner or tomorrow during breakfast?"

6. Plan Ahead and Set Expectations!

Remember right sizing your expectations in Chapter 1? I have learned that if I don't keep my child out past his wall of exhaustion, I'll likely avoid a tantrum. If Carma isn't forced to have long conversations at loud family dinners, she won't break down before her family leaves the house. If I tell my children before we go to Orlando that we're not going to Disney World, they won't cry when we drive by (well, maybe they will, but not as much!)

Planning ahead can include packing tools, such as headphones, fidgets and helpful toys. However, some things in life, like a global pandemic, are totally unexpected, so in spite of the best laid plans of a reasonable parent, children (and adults) may get overheated with big emotions.

A quote floating around the social media parenting space became a mantra for me during a turbulent 2020: "They aren't giving me a hard time; they're *having* a hard time."

My "Oh Sh*t" Moment

Years ago, I was consulting in a kindergarten class. A child in the program was prone to tantrums and had a difficult time regulating his emotions. One day he ran out of the classroom, screaming and crying. A well-meaning teacher tried to calmly talk to him about why he was upset, and he just kept screaming louder and louder. She kept talking in a kind and caring manner, however she had to raise her voice so he could hear her over his screaming.

Then, he started to take off all his clothes. This became what I can only describe professionally as an "Oh Sh*t" moment. Nothing prepared me for this—not my master's degree, a second master's degree in progress, 20-plus years of experience, and raising my three kids. I had no idea what to do with a naked kindergarten kid in the hallway of a public elementary school.

What I did know for sure in that moment was that this child was frustrated, really, really frustrated, and he was having enormous feelings, which meant he was not able to digest any rational talk. We needed to break the cycle of his tantrum and cool him down. I looked at him and asked him if he wanted to watch a video. He stopped, quieted down, and stared at me.

"Come on, follow me!"

I found a computer and a kids YouTube channel and let him choose a clip. While he was calmly watching a video, I helped him get dressed.

We did not sit down with him to ask him what upset him until hours later. It turned out that he really struggled in "centers." After a thorough accommodation plan, he no longer had tantrums during that activity.

In this case, distraction saved the day. The more the well-meaning teacher tried to problem solve with him through words, the more his tantrum escalated. In managing this type of behavior, I recommend the fewer words the better.

Ari's Story

Ari got into a morning pattern of not wanting to get dressed for school. He preferred playing with a racetrack. One day, his mom was prepared for this battle to happen and had some of my suggested tools ready to use.

"Ari, time to get dressed."

"No, I don't want to. I want to PLAYYYYY!!!!"

(Insert foot stomping and crying.)

"Wow, I wish I could play all day, too! But I can't. I'm feeling really slow, though. Hmm, I wonder who can get dressed first, me or you? I think it's me!"

Mom gets up and races to her room. Ari stands there, confused, and then she hears him gallop up the stairs! Playful distraction for the win!

Just like all problematic behavior, tantrums require experimentation. All three of my kids need different strategies for their meltdowns. But a combination of these tricks really works!

"BE A BEHAVIOR DETECTIVE"

BE A BEHAVIOR DETECTIVE- BEHAVIOR IS ALWAYS COMMUNICATION

ALWAYS ASK WHY?

Ask the child? Ask yourselves- what is happening before, during and after. Is it age expected?

WATCH

Some kids need more structure! Are expectations clear?

NEVER TAKE BEHAVIOR PERSONALLY

Is the child missing social cues? Remember rudeness may really be impulsiveness.

CHECK YOURSELF!

Are directions misunderstood or missed entirely?

REMEMBER

The definition of insanity is doing the same thing over and over again, but expecting different results. Keep trying to reach kids in different ways.

REACH OUT

To parents, to colleagues, to your supervisor.

www.faabconsulting.com

Key Points for Busy Moms and Dads

1. The best way to handle, and even cut down or eliminate tantrums, is prevention!

2. Right-size expectations for your kids and plan ahead.

3. Behavior is always communication.

4. Always search for the "why" behind excessive tantrums.

5. Don't be afraid to try something, fail, try again, fail, try again and eventually succeed!

3

Sensory Sensitivities: When Fun Becomes Painful

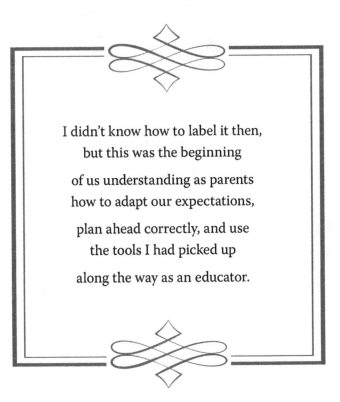

I didn't know how to label it then, but this was the beginning

of us understanding as parents how to adapt our expectations,

plan ahead correctly, and use the tools I had picked up

along the way as an educator.

Sensory Sensitivities:
When Fun Becomes Painful

Disney World is not always the happiest place on Earth. I know this is hard to imagine, but it's true, and an "unfortunate" experience can happen to the best of us.

The Bagdade family version went something like this:

We quickly rubbed the sleep out of our eyes, poured the kids heaping bowls of Fruit Loops, and boarded a Disney shuttle bus. The kids, still too tired to talk, exchanged excited smiles with us as we wasted no time taking plenty of pictures. It wasn't until we drove under the Magic Kingdom archway that the bus full of sleepy passengers erupted with excited chatter. We took more pictures by the welcome signs as we disembarked and were herded into line. Besides all the visual fantasy surrounding you, it's easy to tell you are at Disney World because of the lines, the never-ending lines—for everything.

We waited an hour before the park opened, just like all my meticulously researched blogs and Pinterest pins had told me we would. The kids whined but were easily distracted by the excitement of the day. The anticipation became palpable as I obsessively checked my park app, reminding myself of our itinerary, which I kept sharing with Jeff. I had planned everything ahead of time, taking multiple factors into account, from weather to appetites to shopping, and even room for taking spontaneous photos—all calibrated to meet the expectations of our family. What could possibly go wrong?

Our plan was to run immediately to the back of the park as soon as it opened and do Fantasyland first, before the lines got too long, which they always do, and then work our way back through the rest of the park.

The picture-perfect staff scanned our tickets, opened the queue for us to enter, and off we went—running at first, until we realized we weren't supposed to do that. Instead, we did what Jeff and I came to call "walking in a family hurry," which means you move as fast as you can, loaded down with a stroller and two short-legged humans who can't stop pointing at everything in sight and saying, "Look!" and "Who is that?" and "Where's Mickey?"

We visited with every princess in Disney history and gasped and cheered just as the commercials show, complete with all the requisite "Oohs" and "Aahs" that accompanied every adorable, perfect pose we could manage before posting them by the hundreds on Facebook.

Next, we got in a surprisingly short line for *It's a Small World*. I figured that after our *Pirates of the Caribbean* debacle the day before, where we forgot that we have a kid who is irrationally afraid of the dark, *It's A Small World* would be just what we needed—a welcoming environment of friendly music, laughter and fun—where no one could possibly be unhappy.

As the line snaked inward, Gabi, our little blond bombshell, grabbed my hand when she realized we were heading inside a giant space.

"Mom, will it be dark?"

"No, it's a happy, cheery ride. You will be fine."

I said that with a smile stretched across my worried face, as if that would fool her.

"Mom, it looks dark in here now."

"We are just indoors. Don't worry, Honey. It's not dark."

"Mom, it's going to be dark!"

Her whole body turned into a ball of panic. I felt as if I could see her heart beating through her big, gorgeous blue eyes.

"Mom, it's dark. I can't go. Mom, it's dark!"

I shot Jeff a look. He shrugged and busied himself with our other little one.

"Honey, it won't be scary, I promise. Hold my phone, and you can use the flashlight."

"Mom, she can't shine a flashlight. That's weird. No one is scared of this baby ride. This is embarrassing."

What can you do when an older sister decides to retort like that?

Gabi started to cry, and I quickly distracted her with the iPhone flashlight. Somehow, I managed to get her seated next to me in the small boat that glided up through the water and paused for us. It felt like the Disney gods were there to rescue us with a calm and collected vessel, to usher us through this lazy river to relax and enjoy the ride.

But the Disney gods didn't know Gabi. At every turn, she jumped, shrieked, and recoiled. I smiled, cooed at the baby, as if everything was okay, and reminded Gabi that she had the flashlight in her hand, just in case.

This whole time, during each turn we made from one exhibit to the next, moving in an out of dimly lit areas, my dreams of the happiest place on earth came crashing down all over me.

I understand anxiety. I've worked with kids with extra needs for more than 20 years. I know it's chemical, and I know that my daughter's body is wired to constantly fight these urges. In her case, she constantly feels a bear breathing on the back of her neck, even when it's only animatronic multi-cultural kids swaying to the never-ending sounds of "It's A Small World," trying to convince us for five minutes that we all get along, in spite of our better judgment.

All of this ran through my mind as I felt my own bear breathing down the back of my neck, reminding me that all the prep in the world can't protect you from moments like this. I couldn't help feeling angry and disappointed.

We can't even have fun at the happiest place on earth?
How could this happen when I was so well prepared?
What did I do wrong in a former life?

At that moment, stuck in a cave of singing robots with a panicked child, I was anything but happy. This particular instance was only a reminder of all the meticulous planning I had gotten wrong. I wasn't two steps ahead of my child. Not at all. I hadn't anticipated her triggers and that she wasn't yet ready to self-soothe or calm her own fears. I had failed—again, and my older kid looked at me with her head shaking, undoubtedly adding notes to her list of how she will be a better parent when she grows up.

That night, when we returned to the Embassy Suites, we put the kids to bed. As our oldest and youngest babbled on about the excitement of the day, I listened with relief that we were able to push through our challenges and save the experience for them.

As I bent over to kiss Gabi goodnight, she asked if the rides tomorrow would also be dark. I told her I would double check and that she was safe now. I showed her the nightlight next to her bed, kissed her forehead, and tucked her in.

Jeff and I closed the door to the kids' side of the suite and plopped exhausted onto our bed. We were both drained, disappointed and confused. He looked at me cautiously and I could see him calculating all of his words carefully. That was a good strategy because my patience was at an all-time low, if I even had any left.

"Franki, do you think we should take our kid, who was scared of the dim lights in *It's a Small World*, to Hollywood Studios, where everything is Star Wars themed?"

"But she's obsessed with Star Wars!"

Gabi's fascination with that epic franchise was one of the things about her that charmed the heck out of me. It made absolutely no sense, as she was scared of the silliest things, but she had an uncanny passion for action and adventure, science fiction and "The Dark Side." Pretty ironic for a kid who sleeps with 17 lights on. Maybe she found Darth Vader's voice soothing.

Jeff and I discussed it more and decided to scrap all of our plans for the next day and start over. This was painful for me, as it had taken months of research on Facebook groups, blogs, and websites to get the planning and dining reservations just right.

Our oldest, Ruby, has life-threatening food allergies, so I needed to quickly find safe dining options for her. We decided that Disney's Animal Kingdom, with its historically smaller crowds and mostly outdoor experiences, would be a better fit, initially because it would definitely not be dark.

In a moment of brilliance (if I say so myself), I poked my head into the kids' room and saw that Ruby was still awake, so I motioned for her to tiptoe into our room. I told her that she had been such an awesome big sister throughout the day, even though it had been so hard for Gabi (not entirely true, but she was only eight), so we decided to go with her first pick and change tomorrow's plan to Animal Kingdom. She was thrilled and felt validated and seen. I knew she would have a great attitude for our next outing.

The next morning, I told Gabi the plan and showed her pictures of Animal Kingdom and all the bright, open, well-lit spaces. She agreed that even though she loved Star Wars, maybe she'd wait for those experiences until she was older.

Our two-year-old was excited to see animals. Yea! Thankfully for him (and us), life was still relatively simple, and we all got ready to jump into our new plan, happy for what was coming. We had an amazing day, with short to nonexistent lines, saw great bright and happy shows, and finally got a few good doses of the "happy" experience, which had been promised to us when we first booked our Disney vacation.

I didn't know how to label it then, but this was the beginning of us understanding as parents how to adapt our expectations, plan ahead correctly, and use the tools I had picked up along the way as an educator. That involves reading thousands upon thousands of educational, psychological, and neuropsychological evaluations as part of my work.

It includes learning buzz words, which are used today in the world of children's behavior. *Sensory difficulties. Sensory sensitivities. Sensory processing disorder.*

Sound familiar? None of these concepts are new! Thankfully, we understand far more about the field today then we did in the past. Understanding how your child may be sensitive to sensory stimulation, or a lack thereof, can do wonders for managing their behavior and understanding their limitations. It could also save your perfectly planned Disney trip!

If you want to have a thorough understanding on these disorders, I recommend a book by Carol Stock Kranowitz, called *The Out of Sync Child*, which explains all of the technical nitty gritty about this area. Don't worry; you don't need to be an occupational therapist (OT) or a psychologist to have enough background and understanding to get through to your kids.

I explain these concepts to parents as follows:

We all have senses. Remember the five senses you learn about in elementary school: sight, sound, touch, taste and smell? Let's expand on that a bit, with two senses, in particular. Taste relates to texture on your tongue and the need to chew. Some kids simply don't stop chewing their toys or their pens or their clothes.

Sound sensitivities often begin with aversions to loud noise. Kids are also sensitive to certain noises, the sound of a furnace clicking on and off or a timer in the kitchen. Some kids can't stand "competing" noises, for example, when they are asked to listen to music in a classroom while there is also talking going on.

In fact, that drives me nuts sometimes, too, and I find myself having a hard time carrying on a conversation with a teacher when I'm consulting while there is typical background noise in the room, from students *and* music! (How do these teachers do it?)

It's normal for everyone to have sensory preferences. Those with the actual disorder have more of them and they can become intense, and anxiety provoking and therefore act as triggers for misbehavior. And it doesn't matter if you think they make sense or not!

Ever notice that your child can weep, lash out at siblings and even behaves like a wild animal after a loud birthday party? Events like this can often be a sensory related trigger. Thankfully, we have many physical tools to help children who either become easily overstimulated or who seek more sensory stimulation.

Kids who have *Sensory Processing Disorder* often vacillate between the two. Here are some of my favorite tools for helping when this happens:

Desire to chew: Chewy necklaces, pencil toppers, or water bottles with chewy tops, such as the Camek Bottles.

Noise sensitivity: Earplugs, either wax, or foam, noise cancelling headphones, such as music ones that don't play music or ones used by people working on construction sites.

Desire for heavy pressure: Weighted blankets, weighted stuffed animals, lap weights, vests, heavy sweaters. These can have a calming effect on an antsy, unfocused child and help them with sitting still.

Desire for sensory input when needing to be still: Floam, foam, play dough, silly putty, thinking putty, fidgets, Rubik cubes, Squishies, soft pieces of fabric or rough ones, too, like Velcro circles.

Motor breaks in the winter: Air track surrounded by foam squares, swings, and stationary exercise equipment.

Wherever you're going, plan on bringing a "break bag," even for older kids, so if they need to pop on headphones and take a break from sensory stimulation, you're ready. When children are little, avoid certain situations, as they may not be worth it. Sometimes, we have to ask ourselves: Who really wants this Disney trip—you or your kid?

Some kids are avoiders. They won't finger paint or get messy, and so on. I've had teachers let kids use gloves, add a paint brush, or skip some projects!

I wish I had known many of these things during our challenging trip to Disney World, which became a pivotal "aha" moment for Jeff and me as parents. Some might call it a revelation, while others would say it's a lifesaver that we now know this to be a reality in our lives and we can deal with it and be fine. Either way, facing the truth was essential: *We had a child with extra needs.*

(More to come on that subject in the next chapter.)

In fact, at one moment or another, each of our kids has required extra special attention. During this phase of our parenting journey, our middle child's needs tended to outshine the other two, and she required more of our parenting energy on a regular basis. It affected every moment of our being—when we were awake and when we should have been sleeping. Our lives always revolved around her moods. We worried that our other two kids would feel neglected and frustrated, and we constantly felt as if we were failing, and sometimes they did, too.

By the way, apologizing helps, but changing strategies and making improvements is even better!

To exacerbate the mom guilt further, I was a professional educator and an expert in my field as a consultant for special needs children! That meant I got to be the fun "aunt," flitting from classroom to classroom, offering my advice, helping wipe a nose or two, looking at my watch and thinking, "Oh, my time is up for this month," when it was time for me to leave. In my position, I saw things with fresh eyes that the teachers couldn't or wouldn't notice. I had answers, ideas and solutions for them, but with my own child, all I invariably ended up with was dread, worry and hopelessness.

I needed some expert help!

We had tried a therapist, but Gabi didn't like her. We tried a second therapist, but Gabi refused to go. We tried a third therapist, and when our schedules didn't line up, I took Gabi out of school and took time off of work to meet with her. We were desperate for support but taking our child out of school only amped up her anxiety.

Finally, we found a therapist who was the right fit for Gabi, someone who made us feel supported as parents. Even some of our good work was validated. I was able to step out of the haze with two feet on the ground, get Gabi on some life-changing meds, and remember the essence of what I had learned. It was almost time to plan another trip to Disney.

Key Points for Busy Moms and Dads

1. Take advantage of expert resources if you are raising a child with a sensory disorder.

2. Build a great relationship with an OT (occupational therapist) and/or a therapist to help you with strategies.

3. Teachers can be great resources as well, so don't be shy about meeting with them.

4. Check out my YouTube channel to watch Gabi pack a sensory backpack.

5. Check out my Instagram account and watch my video: *Quick Behavior Tips and Tools #3—Meeting Sensory Needs on a Budget.*

4

Parenting a Child with Extra Needs

Punishing a child who
cannot change his
or her behavior
will not work!

Parenting a Child with Extra Needs

Oh, the joy of home ownership! I try my best to avoid entering our basement. It's the same one we were thrilled about when we bought this house because it was finished and seemed like a perfect place to hide the kids' toys and our collective family mess. Well, as water gushed from the walls during another unpredictable and crazy Michigan winter, the basement became "less finished," and I tried to avoid it for two reasons.

We couldn't afford to re-do it the way we wanted, and in spite of how much I willed it to become true, we never ended up on one of those home improvements shows where they redo your entire house in 24 hours. (Go ahead. Laugh.)

The second reason boils down to one central question: Is the basement actually a mess if I don't see it? I can be philosophical sometimes, and the tree in the woods story, the one about hearing it if it falls, or not, still has me perplexed, so I figure the same approach could work with our basement.

All joking aside, and much to my disappointment, I had to go down there one day to look for something in our storage room. I walked as quickly as I could through the mess I refused to see and came upon the back storage room. A purple smattering of paint caught my eye, but it didn't register until I walked into the storage room and then slowly backed out of it.

Huh? Why are there purple streaks of paint all over the wall?

This was one of the only walls that was still considered finished.

"Jeff, I need you in the basement *now!*"

He came running downstairs, assuming we had another flood, and was relieved to discover that the only catastrophe was the purple mess on an otherwise semi-perfect wall.

"Who do you think did that?" I said.

"Gabi," Jeff said, without any hesitation.

Of course, I knew he was right. We didn't let our youngest one play downstairs without an adult, not yet, that is, and we were quite sure he didn't go unsupervised. That just seemed unbelievable. Gabi, on the other hand, was already in second grade. She was bright, really, really bright, reading many grade levels above her age, and she was excelling at nearly everything. We were good parents. Our rules were clear, and our expectations were minimal. So, what the blankety-blank was going on? Why would our nine-year-old be painting on the walls? Jeff and I went upstairs and decided to talk with her together.

"Gabi, I went downstairs and noticed some purple paint in the kitchen area of the basement. Any idea why that is there?"

"No. I didn't do that!"

Her face started to warm up to a guilty pink.

"Hmm, well, can you stop and really think about it? I know it wasn't Avi because he can only go down there with an adult. Didn't you just spend a few days painting some projects down there?"

"Oh, yeah, now I remember. I forgot I wasn't allowed to paint on the wall."

The rest of the dialogue has been omitted, intentionally, because I'm sure that you are not reading this book to hear about me handling things poorly and yelling and losing my you-know-what. If you don't mind, please use your imagination about everything that happened in the moments that followed this exchange. Then again, I'm just an average parent who goofs up so don't turn me into a monster.

Gabi's words, "I forgot I wasn't allowed to ..." stuck with me for a long time. What did she mean by "forgot?" Is it possible for a child her age to have such a poor memory? Is that normal?

A few months later, I went to a seminar led by Daniel Hodges, a child development expert, about the way boys learn. I found his work fascinating and much of it matched my daughter Gabi more than my son. I told him the story about the purple paint in the basement and asked him how he would approach it. His answer is one I will never forget.

"It sounds like she needs bigger paper!"

Fascinating and simple. Gabi's "misbehavior" was perhaps showing a need she had. So, that year, she got an easel for her birthday. As for the strangely impulsive behavior, we started to see a pattern and it made perfect sense soon after when she was diagnosed with ADHD.

That's when I was introduced to the world of anxious children, impulsive behavior, too little or too much focus and how it all works—not as a professional but as a parent. Let's just say it's been an eye-opener and one I want to share with you.

Quinn's Range of Development

One of my behavioral coaching families had a seven-year-old who had always been sensitive to crowds, noise, and chaos. Since he was an infant and toddler, he cried inconsolably at every birthday party and large family gathering. As a young elementary schooler, he would be the only child who wouldn't separate at drop-off birthday parties.

This was extremely frustrating for the parents. They tried sticker charts, punishments and just leaving and ignoring the crying (the party hosts weren't too keen on that plan!) Yet every time, it was the exact same story. They were embarrassed and angry and ready to stop with the cycle of begging, pleading and yelling.

They weren't too happy with me when we originally met because I explained to them that the problem most likely stemmed from their unrealistic expectations for Quinn. They needed to determine what he was capable of and respond accordingly. If you talked to a teacher or a pediatrician, he was at an appropriate age to be able to separate from his parents and handle some noise and chaos. Heck, most of his friends probably sought out noise and chaos. However, that wasn't realistic for Quinn and who he was at that time.

Remember, child development is all about ranges. By working through some sensory triggers, strategies and tools, he could eventually work on his tolerance for chaos, which we covered in the previous chapter, however, Quinn wasn't ready for this intervention quite yet. My advice to them was to skip some, if not all, of the parties, and to experiment with joining some of the parties for just a portion of the time and having a parent stay with him. Yep, you're right. They definitely wanted their money back, at least for a moment, until they decided to trust my process.

Through the subsequent parent/child meeting (you'll learn all about this in Chapter 6), we discovered that my instinct was correct: Quinn's low threshold for sensory overload was making him meltdown at parties. By following a new strategy, things improved dramatically for Quinn and his parents when they learned to right-size their expectations. (I suppose you've figured out by now why I began this book with the subject of expectations.)

His parents knew that one of them would stay at all birthday events. They experimented with arriving early to make him comfortable before the loud crowd arrived. They prepped him for what to expect as much as they could at each place they went. Sometimes, they left early or arrived late by skipping the main (noisy) activity or joined in just for cake. On some occasions, if Quinn seemed off his game, they didn't go at all and that was okay! If they chose to skip a party of a close friend or family member they would call to explain and set up a special one-on-one playdate instead. However, for classmates whose families they didn't know, they just politely declined the invite. Trust me, parents are typically thrilled to scratch a name off their final list, because birthdays are expensive!

These plans were made ahead of time, collaboratively with Quinn. Now that he has some tools to help him with sensory overload (through a process of trial and error with him, his parents, and myself), he chooses which parties are important to him and he and his family plan ahead. This has eliminated a great deal of stress for everyone.

On one occasion, a child who was really important to Quinn had a party at one of those super loud bouncy-house places. Quinn pleaded to go, even though his parents knew that this party environment would not be a good match for him. This is where Mom and Dad had to explain to him that this would be a parent decision and they weren't taking him. They offered him a special one-on-one playdate with the birthday child instead, so Quinn could still celebrate.

What parent wouldn't be thrilled to have such a kind gesture for their child? Quinn also worked on his sensory sensitivity and developed a literal and figurative toolbox with a great OT and therapist (more about children's professionals in the Resources section.)

What I've learned over the years is that I could take my behavior modifications skills from the classroom and the camp cabin and install them in people's homes. As an experienced educator, I know the importance of setting classroom norms—rules, expectations, or whatever you choose to call them—and what they mean in the short and long term. They must be clear, reviewed and shared. Expectations should always be age-appropriate and realistic for each individual child and shared with any other children (more on this type of interchange in Chapter 8).

One of the most common accommodations I suggest as a teacher/ consultant is to discretely have a one-on-one conversation to explain your expectations with kids who may struggle behaviorally. Check yourself, and make sure your expectations are realistic for that child. Make sure they are clear, and see if they need changes to make them happen.

This same philosophy works beautifully in parenting. If you take a toddler and preschooler to a six-course dinner at a fancy restaurant at seven p.m., you can plan as much as you like, share your expectations with Dora the Explorer as the narrator, and you will still not achieve much success.

But life happens, and we don't always have control. So, when your brother gets married and the rehearsal dinner is like that, expect it to be tough! You'll be less frustrated, and you can plan with your partner to take many turns going outside to walk around with the little monsters!

You may really not like those kids in that moment, even though you really love them.

You may not like your brother, either!

Understanding Anxiety

A therapist once explained anxiety to me in a simple way that really stuck. When it is controlled, anxiety is a good thing. It can provide a necessary and useful emotion, along with a surge of adrenaline. Anxiety is your brain's way of alerting your body that you are in danger and that you better react because there is a grizzly bear behind you.

People with anxiety disorders have "misfires" in their brain, and because their brains are strong and stubborn, they think they "see a bear" and jump into a fight-or-flight response during what seem like "normal" activities to most of us. This can be true for those with a phobia, who are easily scared of heights, darkness, bugs, or even Kermit the Frog (yes, that happened and there's a story there).

In many cases, people have a more generalized form of anxiety with an assortment of triggers. In cases of children with anxiety disorders, they have super-strong brains and are constantly fighting with themselves to move through life. These kids are living among all of us and are often mischaracterized as stubborn, defiant, or something worse.

Guess what? Punishing a child who cannot change their behavior doesn't work! Rewards don't either, because these young people may have no control over their behavior. They may really, really want that toy you promised them if they get all the stickers on their behavior chart, but they may not have the ability to behave in the way you'd like so that they can achieve that goal. It's like telling a paralyzed person that you'll give them a lollipop if they walk.

However, through therapy, and sometimes, medication, children with anxiety disorders can develop coping mechanisms and tools to help them self-talk and regulate themselves. They can also learn to understand their triggers and strive to avoid them.

Parenting these children is a unique challenge. They often need a little extra "room" for their oversized emotions and we, as their parents and caregivers, need to *not* sweat the small stuff. Anxiety can rear its head at any time and place, and it may take the form of anger, snarkyness, or rudeness, to name just a few of its many manifestations.

Ignoring is a really important tool. I didn't say ignorance, so let's be sure we use those two words carefully. Parents need to know what's going on, but their child doesn't always need to know they are being observed and analyzed.

What if you're a parent with anxiety who is parenting a child with anxiety? It runs in families, so this is super common. First, it can be a blessing because you've already walked a mile in their shoes, and you can empathize on a deeper level. If that's the case, then you need to be aware if your kiddo's anxiety is triggering yours. Take care of yourself first. See your therapist, follow your treatment plan, and practice your strategies.

Visualize separating your child's anxieties and yours. I like to put them in different boxes in my head. You can even make a drawing to show how this works. Anxious people can be deep "feelers" and take on the feelings of others. You want to prevent that from happening, as it may very well double your own anxiety.

Like everything we've been talking about so far, prevention is key! You can think through scenarios before they happen and plan appropriate activities. You can right-size your expectations, as they can be different for different kids (see Chapter 8). You can problem-solve together and use fidgets or sensory items, which are useful ways to distract a busy and anxious brain.

Cognitive distractions such as a Rubik's Cube, brain teasers, Sudoku, and reading are great for anxious kids. Any activity that does not allow for multi-tasking will have a better chance of keeping the brain quiet and maintaining your child's equilibrium.

I once had an amazing camper who became anxious in loud crowds. Inside the loud, hot, over-stimulating dining hall, he would eat quickly and pull out a book of brain teasers, which he kept especially to use in that space, and they helped him to reach a point where he actually looked forward to that time of day.

Many awesome meditation apps are now available, as well as Fitbits and smart watches, that remind children (and adults) to breath! A therapist once told me to breath in and visualize a knot in my muscles. Through continual deep breathing, the knot can work itself out. This may work for you, too, or for your child if he or she needs this type of help.

There are many variations on this technique, so be patient and try a bunch of them to see which one is most effective. If none work, don't hesitate to get outside help (see the Resources section).

ADHD

The National Institute of Mental Health defines Attention-Deficit/ Hyperactivity Disorder as a "disorder marked by an ongoing pattern of inattention and/or hyperactivity-impulsivity that interferes with functioning or development." Let's break that down.

Inattention means a person wanders off task, lacks persistence, has difficulty sustaining focus, and is disorganized, not due to defiance or lack of comprehension.

Hyperactivity means a person seems to move about constantly, including in situations in which it is not appropriate, or excessively fidgets, taps, or talks. In adults, it may be extreme restlessness or wearing others out with constant activity.

Impulsivity means a person makes hasty actions that may have a high potential for harm without first thinking about them, or has a desire for immediate rewards, or is unable to delay gratification. An impulsive person may be socially intrusive and excessively interrupt others or make important decisions without considering the long-term consequences.

Over the course of my career, I have seen many children do many puzzling things, then look altogether confused about why they did them! Children with ADHD are often two to three years less mature than their peers. They tend to be quite impulsive, which means many of their actions happen with little to no thought beforehand.

ADHD is complicated and unique to each child, but there are patterns and tendencies that make it manageable for an expert to diagnose and treat. Please do not hesitate to consult a professional if you think your child may need special help. It's not an indictment of them or you! In fact, if you try to deny there is a problem you will never fix it, and you will cause you and your child to suffer a lot more than is necessary.

Cary Does Math

Cary Bell was a delightful child—smart, well-liked and creative. However, Sandra, her mom, felt like she couldn't leave Cary alone unsupervised, even in her own house! One day, Sandra was busy unloading groceries while Cary sat at the kitchen table, doing a math worksheet. Suddenly, she heard Cary's older brother Jaxson shout "Cary why are you doing your math on the wall!?!"

Sandra was appalled and looked at Cary, who appeared equally appalled and shouted back, "Oops! I forgot I'm not supposed to do that!" Sandra screamed and sent Cary to her room.

The next day, I had one of my coaching sessions with the Bells. Sandra brought up Cary's behavior. I asked Cary to explain what happened in her own words. As I watched her collect her thoughts, I had to wonder about a few things.

Did she know she wasn't supposed to draw on walls?

Had this rule been made clear to her?

Did she think about it before she did it?

You may think that all kids older than toddlers know that we don't draw on walls. Well, some kids have difficulty "reading between the lines" and generalizing instructions; they need rules to be laid out clearly and precisely. I asked Cary if she knew that writing on the wall was against the rules. She said yes, but she got frustrated trying to fit all those numbers into a small box on a worksheet, so she forgot!

The late afternoon hours are a hard time of the day for Cary, and she was struggling to do homework after behaving for eight hours straight in school. With that in mind, we added in a motor break before she started her homework, even though Jaxson continued to do his homework right away. We also provided Cary with a huge white board in case she wanted to work out math problems in a big way, but not on the wall.

I told Sandra that if this happens again, consider it a signal that Cary needs a break. She should remain calm and come up with a new solution together, starting with Cary cleaning the wall. Cary knew the rule all right, but in that moment of stress she couldn't slow down her brain enough to remember it.

Right-sizing Sandra's expectations meant acknowledging that sometimes Cary *would* be impulsive, and she should learn how to apologize, fix the problem as best as she can and move on. This way, we set her up for success and reduced the conflict.

Charles in the Morning

The morning can be super tough for Charles. He easily gets distracted while trying to get ready for school. His parents tried having him set out his clothes the night before, but by the time evening rolled around, Charles was already too exhausted from a trying day. He and I brainstormed with his parents during a parent/child meeting (Chapter 6) and decided that Charles should try picking out his clothes for the whole week on Saturday or Sunday afternoon, when he's in a sweet spot, focus-wise, and decisions like this feel much easier. This became a total game changer for him and a great stress reliever for his parents.

Gotta Move!

Only some children diagnosed with ADHD exhibit hyperactive behavior as well. In those cases, motor breaks and physical exercise are super important, utilizing a small trampoline, Dance Party, bike riding, dance, AirTrack, etc. If you live in a climate where outdoor play is not always possible in the winter, create a safe spot inside your home for movement or find an open gym nearby.

Try to get your child to exercise at least once a day outside of school. You may be thinking, doesn't my child just have to sit still sometimes? Well, is that so? Maybe yes, maybe no. First of all, think about the activity and whether sitting is necessary to do it safely. Can your child stand by their plate and eat? Sure. Can they jump and eat? No, bad idea, a choking hazard.

When you do want them to sit, try a fidget or a sensory stimulating toy, like putty. You may even want to try some of the heavy pressure items we discussed earlier. Somehow, the action of stimulating their hands can often calm their body and allow them to sit. In the Resource section, you'll find a list with all my favorites.

In Chapter 1, we discussed having realistic expectations for your children. Let's consider the basics. They're expected to sit for the majority of the day in school, more than they should in my opinion. You want them to be able to comply, for their benefit and so you won't keep having to go to school to talk to their teacher or, hopefully not, the principal.

Considering all the hours they have to keep it together in school—which, don't forget, can take a lot of effort for some kids—expect that when they get home, they'll need to move! You can't expect them to get in the house and immediately sit still for much of anything—except maybe in front of a TV, but is that really what they need?

When your child is little, you can sign them up for Gymboree or something similar, where they can run around and burn off some energy—not a circle-time-centered music class where they need to sit still for the entire time.

I work with an awesome family that purchased a kid-friendly elliptical machine and a small trampoline like the ones made popular for exercising in the 1990's. They keep them in their family room. The parents can instruct their kids to jump on for five minutes as a motor break during homework or they can compromise and agree to some screen time if the kids do it while they're moving on the elliptical!

Win-Win!

Worst Case Scenarios

One of my favorite strategies to use on myself, as someone who was diagnosed with an anxiety disorder more than 20 years ago at the start of my career, and one I also use with kids, is called, "Worse Case Scenario." I ask myself or a child I'm working a central question:

"What are you scared of that is going to happen?"

We want to get to the root of those butterflies in the stomach. They may answer something like the following:

"I'll go to camp, hate it and make zero friends!"

"I will fail my test and get the lowest grade in the class."

"I'll feel so nervous at the party that I won't ever feel comfortable."

They may say something really irrational: "I'll be the one person on the ropes course whose harness fails and I'll fall 25 feet crashing to the ground!" Yikes! We talk each scenario through, point by point. We acknowledge what may not be rational, like the harness failing, and talk about preventions for those situations. We discuss how we may handle the "worst case scenario" and survive it, and what will make it worth trying and pushing through.

Throughout the years, this strategy has helped me and many kids I've worked with, from mild to severe cases. Sometimes it could be the wrong path to take, and the child or adult may not be ready to think through a scenario deeply enough or they may find that this exercise leads to further anxiety. It's important to follow their lead. Experimentation is key when trying to work through anxious habits that hold us back.

Key Points for Busy Moms and Dads

1. Take advantage of expert resources if you are raising a child with anxiety and/or ADHD and build a relationship with a great therapist or educator who specializes in ADHD tutoring/coaching.

2. Ask an awesome teacher for support.

3. If you are an adult with an anxiety disorder raising an anxious kid, this can be a trigger.

4. Don't forget to support yourself with your own therapist and medication, if helpful.

5. Empathy goes a long way. You can relate to someone's struggle even if it doesn't sound familiar or rationale.

5

Choosing Appropriate
Consequences

Ask kids about their behavior!

Their answers may surprise you!

Choosing Appropriate Consequences

"Franki, can you come in here, please?"

"Yeah."

"Our credit card bill is kind of crazy..."

"What do you want from me? The kids are expensive. They keep growing!"

Jeff rolls his eyes.

"I know that! Did you buy a bunch of items for $2.99, like several a day for some reason, from Amazon digital?"

After some investigating, we realized that as first-time parents of the "digital world" our parental controls may not have been tight enough and our eight-year-old had spent $400 on various episodes of her favorite shows. She didn't realize it cost that much because she did it here and there at $2.99 an episode, as if she would have known what it all added up to anyway. When we got out our calculator and added it all up in front of her, she was shocked that it came to a grand total of $400. She was embarrassed and remorseful.

This was definitely an occasion to determine appropriate consequences.

Are You Ready?

Consequences are a funny thing. Most parents, and even professionals who work with children, spend way too much time and energy creating and trying to implement consequences. This is why I haven't mentioned them yet at all, not until we've covered some basics. In my experience, parents are only ready to consider and implement consequences if they have achieved four things, or are at least in the process of doing so, which you are right now:

1. Right-sizing expectations.

2. Implementing parent/child and family meetings, i.e., collaborative problem solving (next chapter) and teaching skills to help prevent problems.

3. Making sure to enjoy their child by spending quality (not quantity) time together.

4. Seeking outside professional guidance when needed (see Resources).

Consequences aren't needed as much as you might think because when kids communicate their needs appropriately, we don't see too much serious misbehavior. More important, we don't want to punish kids for having feelings. Yes, of course we can say things like, "I'll speak to you when you're calm." We don't have to "give in or reason" if they are having a tantrum, but we also don't want to send the message that any emotion beyond feeling happy and satisfied is "bad."

If you are able to follow these steps consistently—or let's say most of the time, as we are human, after all—consequences won't be as necessary and certainly not on a daily basis. That would make everyone feel like they're living in a pressure cooker, and who wants that?

Any time I lead a parenting seminar, a teacher-development group, a training for camp staff, or any program for absolutely anyone who works with kids, I emphasize the most practical and efficient way to handle misbehavior—*prevention*. That's right. This is always true, except of course when misbehavior surprises us in the form of an unexpected tantrum. It happens to the best of us.

Sometimes (okay, most of the time), stressed-out teachers and tired parents look at me as if they wish they had another option. Someone usually suggests an alternative. "This seems like a lot of work. Wouldn't it be easier to use a counting system, or a time out or maybe a sticker chart?" To a question like these, I respond with a story fresh out of my kitchen.

The Bagdade Baking Analogy

If I wake up one day and decide to make chocolate chip cookies and choose to jump right in with the first ingredient, I may realize within a few minutes that I need more sugar. I leave my half-prepared dough on the counter and go shopping. When I return, I notice that my batter looks a little weird from sitting...but oh well, I move on.

Then, oops, I realize that my daughter has used up all the butter so I walk to a neighbor's house and see if they have any extra they can give me. As soon as I get back, I find out that Jeff forgot to buy milk. Do I need milk in this recipe? Yes, I do. Can I replace it with water? No, I can't, unless I relish the idea of my family staring at me stone-faced after dinner, wondering why the cookies taste like sweet cardboard.

I do this for a few hours, handling each step of the recipe as it comes without preparation. Finally, I finish making the batter, turn the oven on and wait a half hour for it to heat up. My 15-minute chocolate chip cookie recipe has now taken me most of the afternoon. They taste pretty good because they have chocolate chips in them, but the texture is off because I kept leaving the batter out to go get extra ingredients.

After taking so long to make these strange-looking cookies, I don't have that happy, accomplished feeling I usually get from baking, because it turned into such a stressful experience and took up most of my day! What if I had approached things differently, with some good pre-planning?

First, I grab my favorite recipe. Next, I make sure I have all of the ingredients I need. Before I start on the batter, I preheat the oven. Thirty minutes later, I'm scooping cookie dough onto a greased cookie sheet and putting them in a hot oven. Wow, the whole process only took about 45 minutes and the cookies spread out nicely and fluffed up perfectly.

Why did that happen? I was prepared! Either way, I end up with a batch of cookies, but by being prepared, strategic, and learning from past errors and success, I produce a much better cookie and a much calmer me!

Asking the Right Questions

Here are some questions I ask myself when my kids and I (or kids I work with) get into a cycle of bad behavior and we have to deal with the consequences:

Have I determined this child's capability, and are my expectations unrealistic?

Have I right sized them?

These questions sound simple, as we have discussed, but they have many levels. Putting a child who is misbehaving on a plan, using an award approach or one that is punitive, will be totally useless if you don't stop and think about *why* the behavior is happening and the capability of that child.

If he or she is struggling with underlying issues, such as a lack of impulse control or poor language skills, communicating what you want them to change is simply not enough! You will have to provide tools for them to improve their behavior. If you skip this step, even the most positively worded reward system will end up being punitive, as the child disappoints you and themselves repeatedly by failing!

Think about it this way. My middle child is near-sighted. She has difficulty seeing the white board from a certain distance. If I hadn't determined this through testing and trial and error, and then provided her with glasses, what would she have done?

What if I had told her to "try harder and I'll give you a sticker each time you can see the math problem," would she suddenly begin seeing better? Of course not. She may be motivated to try, but she would still need assistance from her glasses! And even then, her eyesight may never be as good as someone with natural 20/20 vison.

Consider a child's age. Is it appropriate to expect a five-year-old to behave at a dinner when it goes past their bedtime? Think about who they are. Should I expect my sensory- sensitive 10-year-old to enjoy a loud DJ dance party? What if her cousins are having fun, even, some of the younger ones? It doesn't matter. Expectations have to be right sized for each individual child.

Have I determined the "why" behind the negative behavior?

You may choose not to believe me, but children don't really want to misbehave and disappoint the adults in their life. There are often underlying issues, like a lack of impulse control and/or limited language and communications skills.

Remember: Behavior is *always* communication!

What needs does my child have that are not being met?

What are their frustrations and how can we identify the causes?

There are a ton of different methods to analyze behavior. They all come back to one simple principle: What is happening before, during and after?

Did your child get a poor night sleep before a meltdown? Was he disappointed by a cancelled play date and then got into a wrestling match with his younger brother? Sometimes, the exact trigger is hard to spot. You may want to take notes in your calendar to find a pattern.

For example, Robby comes home from school really cranky, especially on Wednesdays. Let's look at the school calendar. Hmm, he has music every Wednesday before dismissal. He hates music! It is loud and they are in the middle of an instrument unit, which may be really hard for his sensitive ears. In this case, the cause isn't difficult to identify, but finding a solution may be a bit tricky.

In another example, I've been wondering why my happy-go-lucky eight-year-old cries every time he experiences a little moment of disappointment. That's so not like him. What should I do?

Before I jump into "tough love" mode, I need to investigate. What happened right before he was triggered? I can't think of anything unusual. What happened early this morning at breakfast? We discussed the fact that his school was going to move back to online/remote learning. Eric is a people person, and he was devastated by this news. Maybe that's why he's more sensitive today.

When we consider any behavioral issue, we must ask a central question and be absolutely objective about figuring out an answer.

What happened during the behavior "transgression?"

Think about this from a professional detective's point of view. "Charlie smacked his brother for no reason!" is not objective or even helpful. What happened was, Charlie and Ian were playing with blocks. Ian bumped into Charlie, and Charlie's tower fell over. In response to this unexpected accident, Charlie smacked Ian.

Do you see how being objective brings clarity?

What happened after? Did the child get any reinforcement from the misbehavior?

In this case, I spent about 20 minutes talking to Charlie about his feelings. Maybe I need to up my one-on-one time with him, so he gets the attention he needs without doing the wrong thing first.

Am I remembering that the child must be included?

Your powers of observation and having conversations with other professionals, such as your child's teacher, coach or camp director, is helpful, for sure, but if you don't include your child in the process, you're less likely to be successful. Including the person who is having the problem in the problem-solving process is essential! It helps them to "buy in" and work hard with you in implementing a solution. It empowers them!

It's a great time to remind them that they have many amazing strengths and that you are going to use them in helping them modify the more undesirable behaviors. This is also an opportunity to teach them self-reflection skills, such as identifying the issue.

What do they think may help them do better?

What kind of support do they want?

How do they want it?

Who do they want to help them?

Making Consequences Fit the Moment

We have privileges in our household that must be earned by being a responsible member of our family unit. The children are expected to clean up their meals and snacks, keep their personal belongings in the right place, keep their rooms clean and contribute to family responsibilities, such as laundry, taking out the trash, and setting the table.

If they're being responsible in those areas, they get screen time. When they "forget" to fulfill their responsibilities, they lose screen time. Having access to Wi-Fi, TV, and an assortment of devices is a privilege for responsible members of the household. I don't give them an allowance for doing these things, they are expected in our family.

This is a system we have put in place, through a family meeting, including follow-up meetings when things need to be tweaked. When the kids lose screen time, they understand (most of the time) and don't complain about it. I don't really think of these times as "punishment" or "getting in trouble"; they don't happen too often because we're clear about what is expected and what happens if those expectations are not met.

The following text exchange happened between my teen, the same one who rolled her eyes all through our "project responsibility" family meeting. I had to remind her over and over again that she had younger siblings and medication that couldn't be left on the floor.

This was on the floor of the laundry room, I'm taking away a 1/2 hour of screen time

I thought I put that in my bag it must of fallen out when I was getting my laptop in sorry but I understand

If one of our children does something they shouldn't, we typically remove them, if needed, from the "hot spot," especially if they hit a sibling or are screaming at them. That way, they have a chance to cool down before we have our parent/child problem-solving meeting, or if they're still too hot, we schedule it for a more appropriate time. If the behavior has been particularly difficult, I may also use a Jim Faye special: "Daddy and I need to discuss the consequence for this, but we won't be able to do that until you go to sleep, so try not to worry about it."

They will worry, of course, and that can instigate important introspection time for them about what they did wrong. For example, remember when one of our kids skirted our parent settings on Amazon and purchased $400 worth of videos? She didn't realize it added up to that much because she bought them intermittently at $2.99 an episode.

In the end, her consequence was to pay us back. Of course, she had no money of her own, so she had to earn it by doing extra chores around the house We brainstormed ideas of what she could do and designed an appropriate fee-per-chore chart together. It took her a long time to earn the equivalent of $400, but it was an impactful process and it never happened again.

No matter what the "crime" may be, the consequences should be logical. I learned about this model from studying the positive parenting techniques of *Love and Logic*™ and you can find out more about them in the Resources section.

When kids goof up, either because they're intentionally testing the limits or by accident, the event can become a teachable moment; in our case, our daughter certainly learned the value of a dollar! It also helped enormously when we stuck to the facts. This reduces the heat of the moment and makes communication and negotiation easier to accomplish.

As Sergeant Friday used to say in *Dragnet*, "Just the facts, ma'am."

Do any of these sound familiar?

Fact: "You spent Mom and Dad's money and you need to pay us back."

Fact: "You hit your brother so you can no longer play with your siblings."

Fact: "You are screaming at everyone and acting short-tempered."

Fact: "You must be tired and cranky so you should be in your room alone now."

Assessing the facts usually helps to clarify what the consequences should be.

For example, what if two siblings won't stop fighting over a toy? "It looks like you two aren't ready to share this toy, so I'll put it away for today and you can try again tomorrow."

What if your son eats all of his sister's candy? "You need to give your sister your candy or give her $5 to purchase more.

Sometimes, consequences for negative behavior happen organically and a parent intervention is not really necessary. For example, an older sibling is yelling and being bossy while playing UNO with her younger sibling. The next time the older one asks her younger sister to play, she refuses. "No," the younger one says, "I don't want to play with you because you yell too much."

The girls took care of that one without me. Yea!

Consequences should be logical in order to foster growth while turning them into a worthwhile lesson. When our daughter had to do chores to earn money and pay us back, it helped her to understand that earning money involved consistent hard work, which meant that she should not be spending our hard-earned money without permission.

In a preschool classroom, you might see kids turn a toy into a weapon. For example, a tower of Legos can easily become a sword. In that case, what does a teacher do? Pay attention because this could also happen on a playdate in your house. "Oops, toys are for playing, not hurting, so I'm going to put this toy away for now and we can try and use it the right way after we have a snack."

What if in the same scenario the teacher (or parent) said, "Oops, toys are for playing, not for hurting each other, so you can't watch the special movie with us today!" The kid may realize he's in trouble, but he might also not learn the lesson. After all, how does losing a movie connect to making a sword?

Just like our legal system strives to make a punishment fit the crime, parents should also make every effort to connect the behavior with the response. It's up to us to be reasonable and logical in a kid-friendly way. That doesn't mean the consequence will be welcome, but it will guarantee that it's proportional and purposeful. Your child might even end up thinking it's fair!

Key Points for Busy Moms and Dads

1. Whenever possible, consequences should be decided logically: "If you use a toy as a weapon in our home, the toy is taken away for an hour."

2. Consequences should have a logical connection to the misbehavior: "You didn't clean up your paint and now it's all dried out, so if you want more paint, you'll have to replace it with your own money."

3. If you find yourself giving out consequences daily, work backwards and have a parent-child meeting to understand the "why" behind the behavior.

6

The Parent-Child Meeting

Behavior is ALWAYS
communication!

The Parent-Child Meeting

Early in my professional journey, I learned that behavior modification plans, accommodations in the classroom, and a variety of creative communication tools functioned much more smoothly when children were given the opportunity to share their input.

As a teacher, I loved to provide my students with choices for projects so that they could get to know their own learning style and how they could shine. When I became a consultant, I recommended to teachers that they offer their students choices and invite their input. It wasn't long before I observed many great success stories.

As a special education "behavior expert," I often spoke to teachers about disruptive or even disturbing and dangerous behaviors. When I asked them to describe the behavioral patterns, some teachers knew that these behaviors were triggered by transitions, free time, a certain subject, or something more clear-cut like that. Most of the time, though, teachers shook their head and reported no rhyme or reason.

In response to that default mechanism, I would pull out my FBA (Functional Behavior Assessment) tools and my ABC (Antecedent, Behavior, Consequence) chart, as I was determined to find a pattern that could help the teacher and even more important, the student who was at risk. Fortunately, I often found a rhyme *and* a reason, although sometimes that was impossible, given the short amount of time I had to make an effective assessment.

A World of Active Listening

When I transitioned into overnight camping, things moved quickly! The campers changed activities every 50 minutes or so. All of us, the children, staff, and I, navigated more than 1,000 gorgeous acres on foot. Taking days and weeks to analyze behavior wasn't a luxury we enjoyed. Some kids were only with us for ten days and the counselors didn't become fed up enough with their behavior to ask for help until day three!

I watched my colleagues, a group of social workers, do something revolutionary! They talked to the campers and asked them why the behavior was happening. They didn't have to be the "heavy" since the kids knew they weren't the ones to decide if they got sent home or would have to deal with any consequences. As a result, the kids talked to them and were often insightful about their behavior.

For me, this was a "duh" moment! Kids may know why they are "misbehaving," or they may not even think they *are* misbehaving. After all, behavior is just communication, and maybe their behavior was communicating a problem they needed help solving!

I loved talking to kids! I had been in education for more than 15 years before I took on the world of summer camp. I put my own spin on the process and started talking a lot to those kids. I found out quickly, like in a day-and-a-half, that I had to continually modify my style.

I wanted to be taken seriously, because if we had a problem that needed a quick solution, which we usually did, it was because living with 11 other kids in a cabin could be tough and kids (and counselors) only had so much tolerance!

At the same time, I needed my style to be open, which meant being an active listener. If kids thought they were in trouble, some of them wouldn't talk, so I deemphasized the consequence piece and worked more on determining and then solving the problem. I needed the campers to understand what I expected of them, but they also needed to know that we were lucky enough to have tremendous resources and a wonderful professional staff to help them.

I continued to use this conversational style after the camp season ended. That is when I brought campers into my office who had really struggled during the summer. I wanted to determine what kind of support they would need to improve their behavior, adjust more smoothly, have more fun and get along better with their bunkmates.

I repeatedly watched parents keeping an eye on me as they sat next to their child and observed us in conversation. Yes, the parents would chime in, and yes, I would have "parent-only" conversations before and after, but I wanted to give the children the opportunity to be the expert about themselves.

This was so useful I started doing it in my own home! It was remarkably successful there, too. Imagine that. Active listening! It has become one of my passions to teach every teacher I consult with, every parent I work with, camp staff, blog reader and so on, how to solve problems *collaboratively* with their kids. I have even studied professionals who caught on to this phenomenon before I did and have devoured Ross Greene's work, such as *Lost in School* and *Raising Humans*, and *How to Talk So Little Kids Will Listen*, by Joanne Farber and Julie King. Check them out, as they are easy and insightful reads.

Home Meetings

Here is a basic structure of the techniques I use so that you can start parent/child meetings in your own home. The basic structure goes like this:

1. Establish an ideal time. Is your child fresh and calm in the morning or ready for a good talk around bedtime? Find a time when your other kids are busy, and you can have privacy. Include your parenting partner or another caregiver, if applicable. If your child is in the middle of their "negative behavior," i.e. tantrum, back talk, or general super fun obnoxiousness, that is not the right time. I repeat: *That is the wrong time!*

Talking is overrated during a tantrum and it's not usually helpful at all. You and your child must be in a good place to listen to each other and create a plan for change. You may want to schedule this meeting with your child and get their feedback on the time. They may not want to talk to you, so letting them have some control over the "when" will help them buy in.

2. Keep your tone warm and inviting. You want your child to be your partner in modifying their behavior. If you aren't feeling quite up to it and you're concerned that your tone may sound judgmental, angry, or frustrated, that's okay. You're human! However, that should be a warning that it's not the time to have this type of conversation.

Sometimes, it's best to send in your partner (if applicable) for a solo give-and-take, especially if they're feeling less emotional about whatever is going on. They may not feel like doing that, so that could be further confirmation that the timing isn't right. If that's the case, then it's okay to wait until you're ready to do it together. I literally wrote the book on this, really I did, and you're reading it right now, but sometimes my husband is in a better place to have these conversations. Since he's seen me do a lot of modeling, he does a great job, too!

3. When you start the meeting, you may want to see if your child can come up with the reason why you've asked to have a talk, and if so, let them describe it in their own words. When it's your turn to speak, add to it. No judgment. Stay calm, cool and collected. Remind them that they aren't in trouble, that you're just having a meeting.

Ask questions like, "Have you felt like your behavior was any different lately?" or "Have you noticed that I've been yelling more?" Yes, it's okay to admit that you're human, and your child should know that it's okay to make mistakes. Follow that up with, "I really don't like yelling at you, and I know it's not kind, and I'm really sorry. Let's work together so we're both less frustrated."

Modeling this technique enables parents to continually work on their behavior, while understanding the importance of taking responsibility and apologizing. This is a powerful lesson. If your child doesn't know why you want to talk to them, just tell them and be clear about what's not acceptable. You can say this once; that's all it takes, and this kind of meeting is not the time to deliver a lecture. If you determine that your child really didn't know about an expectation or a rule, then your solution may be to educate them. If that isn't the issue at hand, don't spend a lot of time talking about it. Many kids understand the rules but still struggle with them, so there may be another problem going on as well.

4. Be clear about what issue you need to be solved. Try an opening, such as, "Your mom and I would like to have a chat with you about some different behavior we're seeing." Or something like, "Dad and I have noticed that you seem really frustrated lately, and we'd like to have a meeting with you to see if we can help." You could take a different approach by referencing a third party, such as, "Mr. Black called us about your behavior in the classroom. Can we talk about it together?" or "I've noticed that you're very short-tempered with your younger sister lately. What's going on?"

5. Once you've discussed what may be the cause of the behavior (if your child knows), then it's time to brainstorm together on ways to work toward improvement! Maybe your child is over tired, and you need to work on the bedtime routine. Maybe they're getting hungry in between meals. Perhaps homework is getting harder, or something is bugging them at school.

Your child may not be able to reflect on all of this in the moment, so initiating this type of talk lets them know that you want to discuss this with them. It also gives you the opportunity to model an interpretation of our own behavior.

They may have more explanations for you in the coming days. If they don't know, I like to say, "Do you want some ideas?" If they agree, I share my observations, and this typically gets them talking. If they say no, I table the conversation, give them time to think, and let them know that we *will* be talking about it the next time.

6. Use this time as an opportunity to also praise your child on various ways their behavior has been positive, so that the conversation doesn't feel too negative. Maybe you're impressed with the conversation itself, and if so, tell them! You can also acknowledge their willingness to participate in a mature manner!

7. Come up with a mutually agreed-upon plan. Ask your child what kind of help they want from you, and how and when they want it. Then

it's your turn to tell them clearly what you expect them to work on. If they have no ideas, say, "Would you like to share some of my ideas?" and give them some concrete suggestions.

8. Write everything down! Continually review and tweak the plan with them. I often like to review it at the beginning and end of the day. Some kids want their own copy! Others may want to be secretary of your meetings and may even add some artwork to spice up the report. You can also post it on your refrigerator!

A Sample Conversation with a Six-Year-Old

Mom: Hey Buddy, can we sit on the couch and talk for a few minutes?

Sam: Okay.

Mom: I noticed that when it's time to go swimming every week, you start to cry and yell. Dad says when you get in the pool, you are always smiling. He sends me pics and you look happy. I'm a bit confused!

Sam: It's such a longgggggggggggg drive!! And I don't like leaving right after school. When I get home, it's dinner time and then I don't get to watch TV and it's *not fair*!

Mom: Oh wow, that really helps me understand. You like watching TV, don't you?

Sam: Yes, I like to relax after school.

Mom: If only there was a way to watch TV and go to swimming, too.

Sam: Mom, there is!! I could watch it on my tablet, but you don't let us watch TV in the car unless we're driving more than two hours!

Mom: That's true. I like you to talk to us in the car and look outside the window. What if I make an exception, special for swimming days, and you can watch TV either on the way there or on the way home?

Sam: Yes! Please, please, please!

Mom: Okay, I can be flexible, but then I need you do something for me. When you get home, I'm going to ask one time for you to get ready for swimming and I want you to do it nicely with no crying or screaming. If you're a bit frustrated that's okay, but I want you to remember you can ask for a hug or you can hug your teddy to help you feel calm. It's okay to be frustrated and sad, but it's not okay to yell at me and Daddy.

Sam: I can do that, I promise!

Mom: I bet you can! I'm proud of you for being so grown up and solving this problem with me. Thanks Buddy!

Sam: You're welcome, Mom.

A Sample Conversation with a 10-Year-Old

Mom: Hey Izzy, I wanted to talk to you a bit about dinner since it seemed hard for you today. When do you think would be a good time? Now or before bed?

Izzy: Why? Can't we just order pizza??

Mom: We can discuss your dinner ideas later when we talk.

Izzy: Ugh! Okay, fine, at bedtime.

(Later at bedtime)

Mom: Iz, let's talk about dinner now.

Izzy: Fine.

Mom: I noticed you have been really frustrated at dinner lately. You're not really eating anything, and you seem so upset the whole time. You complain, and it's not fun for any of us.

Izzy: Well, that's because I don't like anything you're making.

Mom: Okay, that would be annoying if you don't like *anything* I'm making. I thought you liked pasta, rice and chicken nuggets, and we had one of those things at the last three dinners. What's going on?

Izzy: The chicken nuggets were soggy, and I don't like pasta and rice anymore.

Mom: Hmm, I did make the chicken nuggets in the microwave. Do you think you'd like them better in the toaster oven?

Izzy: Yes! Duh.

Mom: Can you be in charge of toasting them?

Izzy: I guess so.

Mom: Okay, well, I'll make chicken nuggets once a week, but I need other dinner ideas and side dishes. What do you think we can do about that?

Izzy: Can I have extra screen time just to research recipes I want to try with you?

Mom: Great idea! Let's do that on Sunday, and you can help me plan the week! But what do we do if you don't end up liking the recipe and you get frustrated? I don't want to listen to you complaining during our entire dinner.

Izzy: I guess I can keep my opinion more polite.

Mom: I would appreciate that. How about you do that and help me make a shopping list so that you know you'll have a side dish every night that's something you like? That way, there's always something you like to eat. I notice that when you get hungry, the complaining monster comes out!

Izzy: Mommmm, come on, I'm 10. Can we stop talking about monsters?

Mom: Okay! I love you, thanks for problem solving with me. I can't wait to have your help planning meals on Sunday.

A Sample Conversation with a 13-Year-Old

Mazy just turned 13, and her parents are concerned because she only hangs out in her room. She isn't into activities, like sports or dance. Sometimes, they barely see her in the afternoon.

Mom: Hey, Mazy, can we chat for a few minutes? I noticed that you're in your room most days after school until dinner and then again right after. What's going on?

Mazy: Well, I like my room, and it's always so loud downstairs with my brothers.

Mom: You know, we all really missing spending time with you.

Mazy: Yeah, dinner has been gross lately and my brothers are idiots at the table, so I go right back to my room for some quiet.

(I ignore the less-than-stellar language.)

Me: Do you have any ideas on how we can fix this issue?

Mazy: Well, I really like to watch TV on my laptop when it's quiet, and you have parent controls on, so you know it's appropriate. Can I have my own hour of screen time and do my homework upstairs, if I promise that I won't be up there for more than two hours?

Mom: Okay, tell me some more about what that would look like, and when would you be upstairs?

Mazy: Well, I like staying downstairs when I get home and talking to you and having a snack, so how about I stay downstairs until four unless I'm stressed about homework. Then, I go upstairs and do my homework and chill and stay downstairs right before dinner and after for a little while, until I can go back in my room.

Mom: Sounds awesome, thanks for problem solving with me. Let's try it and talk on Friday about how it's going.

A Family Meeting

The other day I was throwing away the 20th goldfish wrapper, collecting water bottles from literally the strangest of places, cleaning up cough drop wrappers from in between couch cushions (keeping it real!) and I started talking to myself.

Franki, it is time to make a change. What would you say to yourself right now if you were your own behavior coach?

When you work for yourself and you're your own boss, you have many conversations like this. I instantly got sidetracked thinking about WWFD (What Would Franki Do) merchandise and wondering if it would sell. Then, I took a deep breath, re-read my own blog article about how to have a parent/child meeting, and got to planning.

1. *Come up with an ideal time.*

I talked with my husband Jeff, and he was instantly on board. We came up with a time that all the kids would be home. We also figured out that no one should be overly hungry or tired or have an activity (not an easy task with three kids).

2. *When you start the meeting, set the agenda.*

Be explicit! For example, I began by calling our family meeting to order, fake gavel and all. Our kids appreciate my flair for the dramatic. Okay, everyone but the tween. I explained that I thought our house was way too messy. I had the kids give me some examples, and we were all in agreement. Jeff and I talked about how we, as a family, are not naturally neat! The kids gave examples of friends they have who keep their lockers and desks perfectly tidy. Avi, my youngest, explained that he had a friend who made his own bed. (Ouch, that stung a little, mom fail on my part, that was so newsworthy).

3. *Keep your tone warm and inviting.*

I infused some grade A Mom jokes with my air gavel! If it works, why not? Humor can do wonders! Highly recommended.

4. *When you start the meeting, see if your kids can come up with the reason why you've asked to talk and let them describe their ideas in their own words.*

The kids did this by helping us come up with a list of parent responsibilities and kid responsibilities. Again, no judgment and no correcting. I just took notes. They did a great job. I took the opportunity for a teachable moment. My oldest, who is almost 13, made sure to get making lunches down on the parent responsibility checklist.

"That's interesting," I said. "I know you want this on the parent list because you don't like making lunches, even though you're old enough to do so. That's okay with Dad and me and we're happy to help you. In order to do that, we'll need help on some of our other responsibilities, so you'll see some additions on your individual chart."

I conveniently ignored her eye rolls and moved on!

5. *When you have discussed what may be the cause of the behavior (if your child knows) then brainstorm ways to work on improvement together.*

We all agreed that no one in our family was a natural cleaner so that made it tough for us. We also agreed that we like a clean house. I proposed that each kid have a list of personal responsibilities, including self-care, keeping their rooms clean and putting personal items away. I suggested that their extra jobs to contribute to a clean home rotate, similar to how they do it in school with classroom jobs.

I also explained that if they wanted to make extra money, I would have a list of money-making opportunities ready for them. If they didn't complete one of their responsibilities, they would owe Jeff or me $2 per job to do it for them.

Our teen was not cool about parting with her money. She came up with a second option: they would lose 30 minutes of screen time for each responsibility they didn't complete.

6. *Use this time as an opportunity to also praise your child on ways their behavior has been positive, so that the conversation doesn't feel too negative.*

Maybe you're impressed with the conversation itself, and if so, tell them! Jeff and I thanked them for their participation in our meeting.

7. *Come up with a plan that is mutually agreed upon.*

Ask your kids what kind of help they want from you, and how and when they want it. Then it's your turn to tell them clearly what you expect them to work on and change.

Key Points for Busy Moms and Dads

Draft a plan for each of your kids, as pictured here. Tweak as necessary and customize it to fit your family's needs. You may notice that this sample is a bit soiled, as "someone" spilled "something" on it before I even hung it up on the fridge. This is parenting in action!

"HOUSE RESPONSIBILITIES"

7

How to Speak Teacher

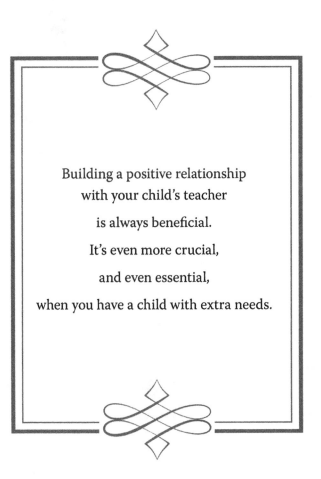

Building a positive relationship
with your child's teacher

is always beneficial.

It's even more crucial,

and even essential,

when you have a child with extra needs.

How to Speak Teacher

Okay, here comes *my* mommy oops! We could also call it a mother's cautionary tale.

My daughter, Ruby, was diagnosed with a serious food allergy in first grade. I was really scared after she had a bad reaction to some cashews. A few weeks later, her class was making gingerbread houses. The teachers asked families to bring in nut-free candy. I volunteered to help. When I came in, I was horrified to see that more than half of the candy had labels that said, "May contain nuts." According to our doctor, this was a big no-no, and when I saw the other volunteers about to put that candy in front of my daughter to use, I nearly lost my you-know-what. Instead of having a calm discussion with Ruby's teacher, I wrote an anxious-sounding email after the party, saying that if I had not been there, Ruby would have been at risk of a deadly reaction.

Because I didn't discuss the situation or ask questions and I made assumptions, I didn't know that the teacher had spent an evening of her free time researching safe candy at the grocery store and asked parents for those specific brands. The requests had not been accommodated, ignoring any safety concern, but I should have worked with Ruby's teacher instead of not accusing her of malpractice. Guess what: we never got that positive relationship back, and when it came time for the end of the year picnic, she asked that I send in Ruby's food because she didn't think she could meet my expectations.

I know. I was disappointed in me, too.

Lessons Learned

What should you do when you are worried about your child academically? Maybe you notice that she cannot do any of her homework independently or her grades may be slipping if she is older. Maybe your child comes home grouchy each day, seeming stressed, or he is able to verbalize that he is struggling in school with his academics.

This can be hard on the child of course, but what about the parents? We worry about our children and how any slip-ups or detours might impact their future success. Whether we like it or not, we absorb the brunt of the stress. Even so, we may end up with a moody kid who lacks confidence and complains about going to school. Then what?

Here are the first five things I suggest when parents contact me in this predicament.

1. Make sure the teacher knows that your child is struggling.

Sometimes, parents fall into a trap of wanting their child's work to be returned in perfect condition, and they unintentionally (or intentionally) do it for them. This doesn't help the teacher to understand your child's actual capability and what type of support they may need. Make sure that homework doesn't come back perfect, or let the teacher know that you corrected it together.

When my child has no clue, even after my husband or I try to help, I may leave homework blank and write a note on top. If a handful of math problems takes you and your kiddo an hour, put a little note on the homework or drop your child's teacher an email. If my child continues to have no understanding in a subject, I always let the teacher know.

2. Tell your child's teacher if you have arranged for a tutor.

Maybe you decided to help your child (and yourself) by setting them up with a great tutor! Make sure the teacher is aware of this. You can discuss this at conferences, on the phone, or through an email. Ask the teacher what topics they should be working on. It's also important to tell the teacher you're providing "intervention" and "academic support," in case you need to make a case later for a 504 (support plan) or an IEP (Individualized Education Plan) for special education.

If you can pull it off financially, hiring a tutor can take a significant burden off the parent/child relationship. That way, you and your child have time to do things you enjoy together instead of having most of your interactions become stressful over homework. Some schools and districts offer this at little to no cost. Sometimes, an awesome high schooler can fill this role at a reasonable fee.

I once was successful in gently pushing a school to test a child they were not as concerned about as I was by emphasizing how much outside support the parents were providing and showing that there were still academic struggles.

3. Partner with your child's teacher and make it easy for them to be honest with you.

I try my best to empathize with teachers. "I'm sure that if I'm struggling at home helping (insert name) focus, it must even be harder for you while you're working with a whole class!"

Check your defensiveness at the door and do a ton of listening before reacting. Some teachers will stop sharing their worries about a child if they're met by an angry parent. Can you blame them? Believe me, they aren't looking for any drama, so leave your attitude in the hallway and be prepared to listen.

Show them that you're all on the same team. Take a moment and put yourself in their shoes. Imagine their day and what they're juggling, because it's a lot. Being a teacher is an intense job and a big majority of them are trying to do what's best for your child.

4. Keep a paper trail!

Start an email folder to keep a copy of all communication. If you talk on the phone or in person, jot down some notes; even better, follow up with an email. This will all be important later if the school needs to take a new approach to your child as a learner. Sometimes, it's important to push for the next steps, including some testing. If your district won't do an evaluation and you'd like to do a private assessment, see the Resources section for contact information on that.

5. Ask for your concerns to be brought up at the next building team meeting.

In Michigan, we call them BIT, the Building Intervention Team. This consists of all the best resources in your child's various school buildings, including Speech and Language pathologists, Occupational Therapists, Special Education Teachers, School Counselors, Social Workers, and District Psychologists.

This places your concerns about your child on their agenda, the first step for the school to decide if they need to provide additional support. Even if nothing materializes immediately from that meeting, it gives your child's teacher a chance to discuss your child's struggles with the experts. It may be that your child just needs a little extra attention from their teacher; let me assure you that this happens through developing a positive partnership!

So how do you build and keep a positive partnership with your child's teacher?

Sometimes, teachers have the privilege of being with our kids during more waking hours than we do. Teachers work hard! And did you know they're also human? Many of them have kids at home and are juggling all kinds of responsibilities, including their own children's homework and school life when they leave the classroom.

If your child comes home with a crazy story about a teacher or something that happened in school, don't assume that it's true! Remember that kids are reporting stuff after a full day with many events. It's totally plausible for them to get parts of the story wrong.

Depending on their age, it may be developmentally expected that they're still working on developing perspective and not exaggerating. In some cases, they may be lying, as this can be a normal phase of experimentation. Young children don't always understand that lying may have consequences, such as when you accuse their teacher of something the never happened!

We teach our kids to be careful about making assumptions, so we should do our best to follow our own advice.

A Teacher's Cautionary Tale

During my first year of teaching, I received an angry voicemail from a parent: "I'm really upset! Austin came home and told me that he needed a plain white t-shirt for tomorrow's class. I'm a single mom and work full-time and it's not appropriate to expect me to provide this with no notice!"

Here's what actually happened: I reminded the class that we had an outdoor field trip the next day and they should dress warmly. I then asked for examples of appropriate clothing. One little girl suggested she wear her new plain white turtleneck under a sweater. Her classmate heard that statement and interpreted it as needing to wear a plain white shirt.

Boy, was that mom embarrassed when I called her back to explain!

We communicate a lot through email these days, which is a wonderful time saver. That said, whatever platform you're using to communicate with your child's teacher—email, text, What's App, GroupMe, or any other app—it provides no way to modulate tone or nuance and your words can easily be misinterpreted.

I suggest calling when you need to talk about something challenging. There's a delicate art to a complicated parent/teacher phone call. When we're anxious about our child and are in full mama bear or papa bear mode, this is tough.

Take a deep breath and say something positive, even if you're super angry and sure you are justified. This beginning statement will set the tone for your conversation. A defensive teacher will not be a good partner and you will not have a productive conversation. I'm positive you can think of one thing that's going well, so prepare for the call and start it with something good.

Examples:

"Charlie is really enjoying your class." (Your child may be even if you're not.) "Charlie loves the book you're reading out loud!"

You can also get personal or even charming and warm, but don't overdo it.

"I hear you're expecting; how are you feeling?"

"Thank you for giving the kids an extra recess so they could enjoy the snow."

Then, jump in with the meat of your sandwich. Ask questions and think carefully about not being accusatory. It just won't help!

"I noticed some of the candy packages had 'may contains' statements."

"Michael thinks that he is supposed to have a new white t shirt tomorrow."

"Randy brought home a 20-page packet of math and thinks it's due tomorrow."

"Piper thinks she heard you tell the class that she was a crybaby. I'm sure that isn't the whole story, so I figured I would reach out."

"Jamie continues to struggle with his math homework every night."

Yes, this can be tough. When we feel that our babies are under attack, it's hard to be the bigger person. But as my dad always said, "Kill 'em with kindness!"

Even if you're confident that the teacher is in the wrong, when you take this approach, they'll want to partner with you and work hard for your child! Also, remember that they're human and may be wrong in one moment and still be an excellent teacher.

If you're not in a good place to make the call, don't do it. Sleeping on it can make a world of difference.

When to email and When to Call

Only use email to ask simple questions or to provide straight information. Your words can be easily misinterpreted, which won't help anyone—you, your child, or the teacher.

"Jack really struggled with last night's homework. I helped him as much as I could, but I'm not familiar with that math strategy you're using."

"Is there a spelling test Friday? Sam wasn't sure."

"Does tomorrow's field trip have suggested attire?"

Any concerns or new information should be shared in a phone call or set up to discuss in a face-to-face meeting. However, please don't give a teacher new information or ask a challenging question when they're prepping for the day. This is a busy time, and the teacher needs the opportunity to be prepared for all of their students. You can, however, write an email to schedule a time for a useful meeting!

Building a positive relationship with your child's teacher is always beneficial. It's even more crucial, and even essential, when you have a child with extra needs.

Key Points for Busy Moms and Dads

1. Check your defensive behavior at the door.

2. Listen with an open mind to teacher feedback.

3. Communicate openly with a teacher about your child's struggles.

4. When it comes to large concerns, email is no place to establish an acceptable tone. Better to arrange for a phone call or in-person meeting.

8

Parenting Each Child Differently

What if I have more than one child

and they all seem to need different things?

Is that even possible? Yes!

It takes planning, but you can parent

each of your children differently.

Parenting Each Child Differently

What if I have more than one child and they all seem to need different things? Is that even possible? Yes! It takes planning but you *can* parent each of your children differently.

This past year, my oldest had her Bat Mitzvah, a rite of passage ceremony celebrated at age 12 or 13 by some Jewish girls. I realized through this experience that because I can anticipate the varied needs of all three of my kids, right-size my expectations for each of them, and plan ahead accordingly, I was able to guide each of them through this big family weekend in a way that each of them needed so that we all could enjoy ourselves.

The first thing my husband and I decided was that it was completely appropriate and expected that the weekend would revolve around our oldest. We were excited for her to experience this, but we knew it would take planning so that the other two would behave and be part of the experience.

With that in mind, we planned—a lot! In fact, it all started three years ago when I picked the date for this event. In the Jewish tradition, when a girl or boy reaches their 13th year, they study to read from the Torah (the Old Testament) and deliver a speech in front of family and friends, which symbolically marks the beginning of their Jewish adulthood. The year leading up to this big day is full of extremely hard work, learning the special musical notes to chant the Torah, practicing reading Hebrew, writing meaningful, personal thoughts and sharing them in front of nearly 300 guests!

That's quite a lot for a pre-teen to take on! In the grand American tradition of "Go Big or Go Home," the ceremony in the synagogue is typically followed by a big celebratory meal and a party in the evening. We started discussing the plans with Ruby three years ago. Always wise beyond her years, she decided that while a big, fancy-shmancy party sounded amazing, she liked the idea of a long trip to Israel where she could walk on the ancient streets and see the history she'd been studying for 12 years come alive. Other than that, all she wanted was a casual roller-skating brunch to celebrate with her nearest and dearest.

Jeff and I were impressed, in spite of what a trip like that might cost.

Sometimes, being the oldest is hard. I say this as the oldest of my brood of three unruly, smelly brothers! I remember growing up and being sent into the kitchen whenever my mom needed help, as if my brothers were totally incapable of lifting a finger, which they were, unless it was going up their nose. Whenever the opportunity to be goofy and misbehave arrived, I was told to set an example and my brothers gladly followed. We always had to worry, however, about the younger ones, who were often overlooked.

"Wait did, we lose Zach again?" That refrain still makes me smile.

Back in the Bagdade house, we focused on Ruby. As selfish as it sounded coming from our 12-year-old, eye-rolling daughter, I understood the need to make the weekend about her. She is an amazing kid, and Jeff and I were happy to celebrate that and make her the centerpiece.

That raised another challenging question: How would we pull that off with a seven-year-old, who doesn't really appreciate the art of sitting still, and a 10-year-old who prefers anything other than the loud echoing sounds of a community service and wearing uncomfortable clothes for two or three hours? The answer required a ton of planning, thinking, overthinking, changing, adapting, being flexible and letting things go.

David's Story

Of course, we aren't the only family trying to keep multiple kids happy underneath one roof. Meet Fred. During the winter, he loves to take his kids rollerblading and share his passion with them for this activity. Tina, his youngest, would blade all day every day if she had the chance! Their oldest, David, always asks to go but then misbehaves and takes on a negative attitude about it, according to Fred and his younger sister!

For a few weekends in a row, Fred really struggled taking Tina and David blading together. Tina and Fred wanted to stay all day. Tina is naturally athletic and is fast and stable on wheels, whereas David, who has been blading much longer, still falls a lot. He loses steam quickly and usually begs to leave before the family is ready. So, most of the time Fred ends up leaving and Tina cries all the way home and begs him to have David stay home the next time.

I facilitated a parent/child meeting with Fred and David so we could right-size his expectations while making clear to David what was expected of him. David shared that he really enjoyed blading, however, he got tired easily and sometimes his legs felt sore, and he needed to rest. It seemed that David didn't have the endurance that Tina enjoyed, and was a little jealous, too. On top of that, David was a bit more sensitive than some kids his age.

Next, it was Fred's turn to explain the expectations. He scheduled one-on-one time for David and told him in that setting that if he chose to go again to the skating rink with his dad and his sister, they would be staying until four. That would include eating a lunch they packed, which, by the way, helps to avoid begging at the snack bar. If David wanted to finish skating earlier, he had three choices, each of which was equally acceptable to Fred:

1. Read a book in the lobby.

2. Spend a half-hour of his screen time on a device.

3. Watch his sister and dad skate and be the videographer.

David loved the plan and added that he would take responsibility for being prepared by downloading a movie to his iPad. He was also able to verbalize through some open-ended questioning that he sometimes gets frustrated and jealous because his little sister skates better, and he just needs a break to cool down.

Saturday went smoothly as David bladed, took a break, and returned to join them on the rink for the next hour. Fred shared with me that it had never occurred to him before to give David breaks, since his younger daughter never needed them, and David was a middle schooler. He now understood that David may always need breaks from things like this, and that it was okay if those needs were communicated and taken appropriately. Fred was learning to right-size his expectations.

As the brilliant Ross Greene has taught us: "Kids do well when they can!"

What I Learned

A couple of months ago, not long before Ruby's big day, I was in a toy store with Avi, my youngest child. While he was involved staring at a display, I found a few small toys of interest that he and Gabi could open before the weekend started. I shared this with Ruby, who thought that it was a great idea, and she asked if she could be the one to give them to her sibs. One might call this a bribe to get these kids through two hours of pictures and sitting still more than they'd like, but I prefer to call these presents *motivators*, which also gave Ruby a chance to show her appreciation to her younger sister and brother.

Those gifts certainly came in handy as we got ready for taking photographs and Gabi had a major meltdown about the outfit she was supposed to wear. She had pre-approved the dress, but when it came time to wear it, she swore it didn't feel right. Here is where "let it go" comes in to play. I loved the original dress; it was so cute, and I had bought it on sale, so I loved it even more. After a bunch of hoo-ha back and forth, Gabi found a plain, clean, black one that still matched her accessories, I had to move past my desire to control her choice and the disappointment I felt when she rejected the one I picked.

That's what "let it go" means.

My son watched this unfold and tried to change his outfit, too. He is not sensitive to clothes the same way, so I said no, firmly, and ended the discussion before it has chance to even begin. See? We can parent different kids in different ways. Fortunately, this was a realistic expectation I could make for Avi, and he relented without any struggle.

As many families know, when it comes to documenting big events, developing a solid strategy for photographs is crucial. We worked with the photographer a year ago to spread out the schedule. We took the bulk of them, including the ones with siblings, the night before Ruby's Bat Mitzvah.

That meant we had to get dressed up twice. I know, I know, but let me tell you, the mood of those two jokers after two hours of posing would not have been ideal heading into the sanctuary for the service. This was about defining appropriate expectations, even though it created more work for me with two sets of pictures. One thing I tell parents all the time is to make sure their expectations are right-sized and realistic for the age, development and needs of your children.

Easier said than done, right?

On the way home from the photo shoot, I was thinking about how long I had been planning this event and that the picture-taking had been a mild disaster. How could I blog about this now? How could I call myself an expert on behavior, children, and parenting? I felt like a fraud and didn't think I would ever be successful. All this super rational stuff going on in my brain was getting me nowhere fast. Jeff looked at me as if he read my mind perfectly (one of the perks of a great marriage).

"Wow, Franki, you did a great job organizing everything and planning the pictures."

I smiled at him and thought about it again. Yes, Avi whined for the first twenty minutes so we had to retake a few of the beginning pics, and yes, Gabi was not wearing the original dress. There had been some complaining (maybe a lot), but Jeff was right. We took two hours of pictures with siblings, grandparents and cousins. When we look at them in 30 years, maybe we won't remember the whining and the last-second costume changes.

Honestly, though, in the grand scheme of things, their behavior was expected, at least by me. That's why I planned to take the pics the night before in the first place! I can't speak for the photographer, but they must have special patience training.

On the morning of the Bat Mitzvah, I knew we'd need at least a half-hour of pictures with the clergy and some last-minute time to get ready. I had our most favorite babysitter in the world come to our house early to give Ruby's sibs lots of attention and drive them to the service just on time, so they were not already annoyed and fidgety when everything started.

Remember how this weekend was all about Ruby? Well, this Jewish star was really nervous on the way to the temple so having the undivided attention of both of her parents was awesome for her. She even gave me some pity laughs as I suggested we make a run for the Canadian border, located just a half-hour away from us, if she decided she really could not go through with her Bat Mitzvah.

The other conscious decision Jeff and I made was to focus on our family of five before thinking too much about all of our other family and guests. Therefore, we decided not to do a family dinner Friday night or a lunch after Saturday morning services. Some families love to go, go, go and that doesn't bother me much, but I only represent one-fifth of our family. My kids and my husband need down time to veg between events where they're expected to behave.

Ruby needs the most home time of all, so she was thrilled to go up in her room and chill after the service was over and the pressure was off, as she loves to decompress by herself. I'm proud to admit that we hit a home run with her on right-sizing expectations.

I asked our babysitter, who is a member of our family at this point, to sit with Gabi and Avi during the services. This made my middle, anxious kiddo secure that she knew who to go to if she needed something. All she had to do was turn to her right for whatever quiet little toy and fidget she wanted, which did wonders to keep her quiet and calm throughout the service. Bringing our devoted and wonderful babysitter was the best decision we made.

The kids were all utterly amazing that morning. Somehow, Gabi managed to have a Rubik's Cube in her hand when she went up to the Bimah (the stage where all the action happens in a Jewish temple), and I'd like to think that God and my dad had a good chuckle about that one! Watching Avi and Gabi hug and squeeze Ruby and the pride on their faces made all the planning totally worth it!

Did I mention that I even thought to bring Kleenex to dab away the tears that came rolling down my face? I sure was glad I had them on hand.

When it came to explaining my expectations to our kids, I spent a ton of time over the preceding months, weeks and days, explaining everything to them—my decisions, why and when things were happening and what I expected of each of them in each moment and especially during transitions. I also praised them at each step along the way, ignoring anything negative and reinforcing everything they did well. This wasn't easy! I wanted to address the meltdowns that happened over nothing, and I was inclined to yell and lecture, but I took a deep breath and celebrated the fact that those hiccups were just that—hiccups—and we were able to move on.

On Sunday morning, I decided to have Jeff bring Gabi and Avi in a separate car to the roller-skating party. This meant fewer cute Instagram perfection photo ops of us in our coordinated donut decal retro outfits, but it also meant more rested siblings who were eager with anticipation when they arrived, instead of dreading hours of pics! Our amazing babysitter came early to make sure Gabi and Avi were happy and well taken care of, and she made sure they took a break from roller skating and ate some real food! Once again, she was extremely helpful and allowed me to genuinely enjoy the party.

At the end of the weekend, Ruby thanked us so sincerely that for a minute I could have sworn she was my sweet six-year-old again and I forgot that she was a champion eye roller and soon to be 13 years old! The weekend was perfect in all its imperfections, and I cannot wait to do it all over again in two years with Gabi!

Structures and Expectations for Different Kids

Gabi and Ruby get dressed first in the morning. Then they eat breakfast and catch the bus. This works for them, and they make it on time. Avi wakes up starving and needs food right away or else he has a fit. That means he comes downstairs in his pajamas and is able to easily transition back upstairs to change and get ready. Gabi requires some extra attention, so I work that into the timing of the morning.

This is a structure we set up years ago, collaboratively with the kids, and it works. In two years, when Avi moves to an earlier start time at school, we will sit down together and plan a new schedule. Perhaps by then, Gabi will have a new set of needs—or maybe fewer, if we're lucky.

Ruby had an extremely controlled, over-monitored Instagram account when she was 11 years old so she could stay in touch with her cousins. Gabi has not shown the same maturity, so she has not yet received this privilege at the same age and will likely not enjoy that privilege until high school. Conversely, she has three days of after-school activities while Ruby has little to none because she needs more down time and sleep.

This is where having blanket family rules may hurt you. Once again, it's important to right-size your expectations for each kid and handle their needs individually.

Key Points for Busy Moms and Dads

1. You can parent different children in your house differently.
2. Right-size your expectations for each child.
3. Your kids may be ready for different privileges at different ages. Same for struggles.
4. Child development exists on a spectrum.

9

Learning to Enjoy
Your Child Again

I love my kids, but I don't
always like them!

Learning to Enjoy
Your Child Again

When it comes to liking my children as much as I love them, one essential tool stands out and remains an imperative. Each day, I enjoy my time with each of them and make an effort to fill up our "good feelings bank account" on a regular basis for when something becomes difficult, which is guaranteed to happen. This is something we work on intentionally in our house.

Considering the six-year age range of our three kids, it can be a challenge to spend quality time with them together. We now realize that there are two things they all like to do. They love family board games and building toys! My mom started an awesome tradition several Hanukkahs ago and buys them a "group gift" they can enjoy together. Our favorites have been a huge box of board games, snow play with sleds, a snowball shaper, a brick maker, a snow painting set, a mini foosball/air hockey table and a classroom set of Playstix. Is that enough to get you started?

We have dedicated many birthdays and Hanukahs to building an impressive collection of family group activities. Really, we could start a YouTube channel with training films on how to pull these off and have loads of fun. Stay tuned, because you never know...

I also have found special things to do individually with each of my kids. With three of them and two working parents, this is never easy. That said, with some creativity and a ton of planning, we can always make it happen. It doesn't have to be an outing and it doesn't have to cost any money. It could be a 15-minute round of Go Fish! with just one kid or spending extra time with them at the end of the day, lying in their bed and listening.

There's that listening thing again—always a welcome activity if you can get a kid to talk. In addition, like many things in life, if I invest the time upfront in one-on-one time, I end up spending way less time managing meltdowns and misbehavior. I consider these sessions as a good investment.

Avi likes to play games with me and will run any errand just to hang. Gabi wants to go out to lunch (if she can bring her Rubik's Cube), and Ruby likes the finer things in life, which I won't detail here, in case she reads this and gets any ideas. We enjoy girly things together, like pedicures, nice haircuts and virtually anything that includes chocolate. When the pandemic hit and all our favorites were out of reach, I found us bonding the most as we drove to allergy shot appointments and the office waiting room turned into our car.

There is no "right" formula for the timing and frequency of this intimate time. I find it works best when I'm truly listening to my kids and being observant. When my 12-year-old whines that I'm looking at my phone too much, it's time to hide it from myself (yep, I do this) and talk with her, using actual eye contact, à la the 1990's. You should try it sometime; it pays big dividends.

When my son complains that he never sees me, I know it is not about quantity, even though sometimes he says that when I haven't had any late work nights or early meetings in weeks. I know this means he needs me to play with him and truly engage. In all honesty, I don't usually want to. There, I said it. That's because it's hard for me to slow down my brain enough to enjoy UNO. Also, sometimes I'm just spent (I wonder why) and I'd rather be scrolling on Facebook. Despite that, I make myself connect with him and I always enjoy being in the moment!

When I find myself worried and frustrated with any of the kids, instead of laughing and enjoying them, I up the quality time I spend with them. It works!

If you're lucky enough to have a strong parenting partner, share in this because when it's clicking, nothing is better. Jeff does a great job on the weekends, taking them to sporting events, riding bikes, and skiing. These aren't my idea of fun, so he takes the reins on those, and I do different things, like a leisurely walk around Target—with our kids!

If you have them in your life, grandparents can offer your kids great attention too! When you have a child struggling with behavior problems, it's important to stay focused on their strengths instead of their deficits and focus on these when planning an outing or a little quality time at home.

It's also essential to help our children build a social identity outside of the family. For many kids, this comes easily, and playdates will do. Some kids struggle in the social jungle, however, and need some instruction in how to navigate that territory. Either way, the fun part for me is when our kids venture out of the nest for a moment, only to return and appreciate the comfort zone of home and the love of their mom and dad.

Learning to Like Penny

This story was told to me by Chris, the mother of a young teen named Penny, whom I worked with on behavioral coaching. Chris now problem-solves with her daughter on a regular basis, and she called me excitedly one morning to tell me an adorable story. She began by sharing some of the changes they had made in their house to work together to meet Penny's needs! Chris was so excited to know that she not only loved her child, but she could like and enjoy her, too!

Here's the story, according to Chris:

At six-something this morning, a child climbed clumsily into my bed. I was awakened by the movement. Assuming it was my youngest, who felt he'd been chosen to fill in my husband's side of the bed the minute he vacated it to get ready for his day, I smiled and dozed off for a few additional minutes.

When my alarm went off for the second time (okay, fourth), I turned it off, rolled over and spoke to my son, still half-asleep. "Hey, can you go make sure Penny is getting in the shower?" Imagine my surprise when I heard someone else's voice.

"Mom, it's me!" Penny said.

Having my daughter climb into bed with me didn't happen, at least it hadn't for a long time. In fact, I can't remember the last time she did. See, we were almost always at odds. I think we feared each other and certainly weren't able to please each other. She was so unpredictable with her behavior. In fact, all our arguing and negotiating left me depleted by the time the evening rolled around. I loved her something fierce but liking her and enjoying her wasn't easy. This was a source of constant guilt.

Somewhere along the way, my way more even-tempered husband started to take over bedtime. He still had patience for the kids after seven p.m., and by that point was much better at giving them love and attention than their burnt-out mama. In fact, now my kids only want to be put to bed by Daddy! You know what, that's A-Okay in my book!

It's been wonderful for all of us. Penny and Doug are very Mommy-attached and fought about who could sit next to me at restaurants until Penny turned 12. That's why giving up favorite status for a chunk of each day has been super healthy for Charles and me. This progress didn't happen overnight, though; it took many steps.

As I listened to Chris tell her story, I realize that she and Charles had right-sized their expectations for Penny in her development as an upper-elementary-schooler, and then as a middle-schooler, with deficits and areas of extreme strength. They also stopped being annoyed, embarrassed, worried, and frustrated when she didn't do things they knew she wasn't yet able to do. They had the expectation game under control.

A great example of this was their coming to terms with Penny's somewhat negative personality. When Chris picked her up from an activity, even one that she was confident that Penny enjoyed, she often started with the negatives. After several parent/child meetings, Penny was able to verbalize that group activities exhausted her more than others. She was often physically and emotionally wiped out by then and needed time to decompress.

Her mother's well-intentioned questioning felt overly abrasive when Penny was on overload. Chris now implements this system for school, birthday parties or after activity pick-ups. At those times, she is careful not to barrage Penny with tons of questions when she gets into the car. If Penny says she doesn't want to talk about whatever might be happening, Chris complies right away. This wasn't always easy for her, as she is someone who enjoys immediate feedback, especially when she dropped Penny off at an expensive activity.

If Penny's response is 100 percent negative, Chris and Charles give it scant attention, instead opting to say something supportive and validating without encouraging any further complaining. Then they change the subject. They may say something like, "What a bummer, Penny. Do you want the radio on or off?"

When we originally worked on this plan, Chris asked me a pressing question. "What if the negative feedback is really important, or what if something was actually wrong? I don't want Penny to have the Girl Who Cried Wolf syndrome." I assured her she would know. She shouldn't discourage feedback from Penny. Instead, she could assure her daughter that she was in the right mindset to share it.

Most often, Penny's positive comments on parts of the activity come out later when she's had time to decompress. I gave Chris a few suggestions for what might help Penny calm down and communicate if she comes home continually complaining and whiny. These are specific for Penny but can easily be adapted for other kids in need.

1. Sit in her swing and read. I suggested an awesome, hammock-style swing in her room, which is a great tool for when she's overstimulated.

2. Use some screen time as a distraction.

3. Do something active, such as dance, ride her bike or even sit on the front porch in their rocking chair and listen to music.

Chris and Charles are trying to make things better at home, and in my opinion, they're making good progress. For example, if Penny starts crying, they don't give her a choice about going to her room. They still validate, ask her if she needs a hug, spend a few minutes listening, and then remind her that she calms down most easily in the privacy of her room.

They are careful not to send the message that crying is not okay, because it is, and it can be a useful release. However, while a child is melting down and sobbing is not the best time for a conversation. When Penny is calm, her parents are available to hear her out for as long as it takes. Sometimes, Penny doesn't cry but keeps retelling negative stories.

That's when I pulled out a favorite camp activity that focuses on reframing a conversation. "Roses and Thorns" worked beautifully for Penny and her parents. The idea is simple: roses are beautiful and positive, and even roses can have thorns, so for every two thorns Penny shares, she must come up with a rose.

I also suggested they try "Stars and a Wish." Stars are the positives, and a wish is something negative that is reworded positively. For example, instead of "the kids were so loud and annoying" Penny would say, "I wish the kids had been quieter."

Some kids work so hard to "keep it together" when they're away from home that parents receive an overwhelmed, overstimulated and exhausted child at pick-up time. In my years as an assistant director of a large overnight camp, I used to get panicked phone calls right after a session pick-up from parents, telling me that their children had nothing positive to say about camp!

I knew these kids and had enjoyed the pleasure of watching them smile, grow and enjoy themselves for anywhere from ten to 24 days, so I would remind the parents that sometimes kids need space and time before offering feedback, and that I was guessing the positive stories would start trickling out when parents stopped incessantly asking. It worked every time! Of course, if a child persisted in their negativity, we would look at it more closely, as we did with Chris and her fear about the Girl Who Cried Wolf.

Why is this story in a chapter about getting to enjoy your child again? It's simple, really. Having realistic expectations is key in this battle. Sharing parenting responsibility and "favorite status" can be helpful, and having a plan, like Chris and Charles did with Penny, can go a long way.

Now, Chris and Penny can enjoy an early morning cuddle.

Another essential tool for "liking your kid again" is to plan ahead and to do it consistently! When you have a child with extra needs, being one step ahead of them consistently saves you from constant aggravation.

Chris and Charles do this with Penny's input. They have separate parent jobs and Penny jobs. For example, Penny always keeps a "sensory tool kit" in a purse or backpack she wears and has one in the car that helps her to be in a more positive place if she's not at home with access to her normal comfort zones. Penny is responsible, with parental reminders, for packing this with fidgets, headphones, thinking putty, and a drawing pad.

Chris and Charles are now able to call a parent/child meeting when Penny's behavior gets sloppy or a new issue emerges. They follow the same basic structure each time, being careful about the best time of day to hold these meetings. They also use the same basic structure to call family meetings, such as when they see a negative behavior with all their kids, which could be not cleaning up after themselves, negative attitudes, not being kind to each other, and so on.

Patricia's Story

For Patricia, one of my favorite clients, gymnastics has been her key to social success. In fact, gymnastics has become her outlet for everything. It gives her the movement and exercise she craves for nearly 10 hours a week. It provides needed structure when the school day is over.

Time out of the house that is all about her is something she really craves as the oldest kid in the family. She feels confident as she excels physically on the mat, and she finds the social jungle way easier to navigate when she is with children who share the same interests.

Years ago, I was lucky enough to hear Temple Grandin speak. She is an autism advocate, expert, and author. While she was focused on autism, her advice for those who didn't find it easy to make friends was more universal. She said to find something, anything at all, that your child enjoys, and make sure they join a club, class, or other activity surrounding it. That is where they will find their people. Great advice.

This could not be more appropriate for Patricia. She has found her tribe, and for that her mother is constantly telling me that she will be forever grateful. Why is this important? Sometimes, part of enjoying your kids more is creating a little space between you and them. That was needed in this family. It also helped Patricia build her self-esteem, which made her much more enjoyable to be around.

Taking Care of Me

Doing the hard work of remembering to do my job of right sizing my expectations and making them clear to my kids has gone a long way in liking my children more! (Yes, I'm human, and this is hard for me, too.)

Taking mommy time-outs (I sometimes lock myself in the bathroom for three minutes of peace) is crucial, and walking away when I'm fired up has become essential.

When I take a deep breath and steady myself, I'm able to remember my toolbox and make the next move with compassion and understanding. I talk a lot about Mom-Care, me time, and self-care on my social media channels. Why? Because I don't have it all figured out yet, but I do know that it isn't a choice; it's an essential part of being a good mom.

Loving my kids has always come easily, but on some days enjoying them is a bit harder. We need to constantly check our balance. When we find that we're approaching most of our parenting time with dread and trepidation, we must first remember that it's okay.

I've been there! All your friends, whether they admit it or not, have too! Take a deep breath and try a new approach. Remember one of my favorite quotes: "Insanity is trying the same thing over and over again and expecting different results."

PARENT TIME OUTS

Key Points for Busy Moms and Dads

1. Each of us parents must find our way to spend quality time with our kids. What do you do to secure that in your house? What might you add in the future?

2. Are you customizing activities for each of your children? If not, what's keeping you?

3. If you're not sure about what each of your kids really wants to do with you — ASK THEM!

4. Of course, being children, any and all of this is subject to change, so keep this whole process fluid, and enjoy it!

10

Let It Go

Harness your inner Elsa
and LET IT GO!

Let It Go

As you know pretty well by now, I have a sensory-sensitive child named Gabi. She is strong-willed. My dad would have called her a "stubborn Hungarian." We have battles over many things, and I continually remind myself to pause, breathe, and let it go. In other words, "Franki, pick your battles." It took me two children and many arguments to get to this place.

When I realized I was arguing about socks at least three times a day, I had an "aha!" moment:

What if she didn't wear socks at all?

What would be the actual consequences?

Could she survive a Michigan winter?

Maybe no socks would stink up her shoes.

If so, is that fixable?

I think so.

I type "shoe smell spray" into my Amazon search box.

Maybe her shoes won't feel comfortable without socks.

Would she learn something from that experience?

Is what I think is comfortable the same as what she thinks is comfortable?

Would not wearing socks go against societal norms?

Would anyone notice?

If they did, do I care?

Would she care?

Would it change everyday life for either of us?

Well, actually, yes.

There may be one less thing to fight over.

After this process of incessant thinking out loud, I made a choice to let it go. It became the stubborn Hungarian's choice whether she wears socks or not. It seems uncomfortable to me, but it suits her just fine and it's one less step to getting dressed in a normally hectic morning. We're going on close to ten years now of no socks, except for skiing and bowling.

Hopefully, this choice will not affect her ability to get into college.

Years later, when my youngest was a toddler, he forgot to wear underwear most days. I asked him what kind of underwear he liked and let him pick out new ones. He still "forgot" most days. I could dig my heels in and send him back upstairs, slowing us down and dialing up my aggravation during our race to get out the door. Or I could let it go. I chose the latter.

By the way, one day he simply stopped forgetting!

There's a Reason for Some Things

Sometimes, when kids argue about socks or underwear, they're genuinely sensitive to fabrics and fit. Sometimes, it gives us a clue that they may have a sensory disorder, or they may just be exercising control. Young kids like to experiment with this, and often feel they don't have much autonomy. Either way, this typically bothers parents more than kids.

In my last year as an assistant director of an overnight camp, I heard a story about a new camper, just seven years old. His counselor was appalled that his parents forgot to pack him underwear—poor little guy! When our unit head called them to request that they ship some, the mom just laughed.

"Oops," she said, "I forgot to tell you he doesn't own any. He never agreed to wear them." This little guy was one happy camper, underwear not included! Bravo to his mom for "letting it go!"

This made me think about what other needless battles I was fighting as a mom, as an educator, and as a professional working with kids. It's important with kids to pick your battles, especially with those who have extra needs. These children may often be skilled at arguing with you. In fact, I bet most of these kids are going to be amazing, strong adults and continue to give us grey hairs as parents! So now, I ask myself three essential questions when I'm about to argue over anything with a kid.

How important is it?

Who is it important to?

What are the positive and negative consequences if I let it go?

Here's an example of what happens in our home when it comes to clothes. It begins with a few basic questions, because once again it's all about perspective.

What would happen if their day-to-day play clothes didn't match?

Do I care if a parent or adult is feeling judgmental about my kids matching abilities? Are they possibly judging me instead of my kid, and do I care about that?

Nope, nope, nope. Not at all. Three big fat noses, as I turn up my nose with the word no.

If one of my kids has a nice event to go to, I pull the "this time it's my choice" card, but otherwise I try to buy them bottoms in neutral colors so that they can't clash too much. I focus on the positives. Their clothes are clean; they chose them themselves, and they got dressed.

When it comes wearing t-shirts in the winter and not dressing for the weather, I approach this as one of life's ultimate teachable moments. For example, if a kid wears a t-shirt to school and feels cold, the next day that kid will wear a long sleeve shirt. Voila! Obviously, when we have negative temperatures, we must insist on a bit of protection, but a little logical life lesson for my kid? Where do I sign up?

When they were little and I didn't want to deal with this battle, I just removed the t-shirts from their room during the winter so they were no longer an option. They just disappeared and magically returned in the spring.

Another thing I often do is throw a sweatshirt, gloves and a hat in their backpack, tell them they're there, then don't talk about it again.

They'll grab them if they are cold enough or when they see their friends put them on for recess.

How about wearing PJs to the grocery store? Is that appropriate? I've been known to shop in my sweatpants, but at least we have groceries in the house. How about wearing rain boots without rain or snow boots with no snow? Did your child put them on herself? If so, you win! These are just a few examples of ways we've simplified clothing issues in our home and intentionally avoided any major power struggles.

A mom I worked with told me that the strangest snack her son loved were frozen waffles. "Do you mean Eggos?" I said. "What's so weird about that?" She then went on to explain that he couldn't wait for her to toast them, so he ate them frozen. Weird, yes; dangerous no. Maybe she just discovered a new cure for teething.

Here we go again. By right sizing your expectations, you're in essence letting things go. You may have a child that won't behave after eight p.m.; therefore, you don't keep them out after that time—if you do, you don't get annoyed if they whine. You may have a child who hates birthday parties, so you send back a polite "thanks but no thanks" reply and send a gift.

That's right. Let those parties go!

Do Yourself (and Everyone Else) a Favor

Letting things go is equally important as the kids get older. School has not come easily for my youngest. He can rattle off facts about transportation, baseball, or animals like no one else, but ask him to write a paragraph and he turns into a puddle of tears. Thankfully, he still loves school most of the time. He's a social little man, and he loves his classmates and teachers. He still loves to learn new things and to ask and answer questions. He works extremely hard because many grade-level tasks challenge his natural abilities.

When we were fighting and he was crying every night about homework, I worked with his teacher to reduce his workload. He was more exhausted than others at the end of the day because of his learning challenges.

Guess what? He never learned cursive. (Insert audible gasp!) I know. What was I thinking? Well, I'll tell you. I decided that not being able to write in cursive was better than having a relationship with his mom that was all about tension over his homework. I decided that not being able to write in cursive but preserving his love of learning and school was better than the alternative. This time, I determined it with his learning team, and we all decided to let it go.

Now, we finally come to the beast, the one every parent has to deal with, unless they live without any screens in their house. Full disclosure: I'm a parenting expert, and I (deep breath) don't know the best way to limit screen time for my kids without yelling at them and whining and complaining about it. There, I got that off my chest.

So, you know what I do? I keep trying. Every darn day.

A few things have worked. I use the free setting on my smart phone to control their screen time. I limit their time on apps (mine, too), and the phone shuts down at eight p.m. every evening (except for the call feature and a few others.)

When my oldest became a teenager, she started missing out on some communications about plans because her friends don't text or talk on the phone. They "Snap" and DM and do other things that confused this middle-aged mom. Ruby and I had a long, calm talk about this. I decided to try giving her way fewer limits on these apps then her younger siblings.

Surprise, surprise. She still did well in school; she was still well rested, and she still had non-tech hobbies. I decided to get over my fear of the evils of screen time and not create a problem that didn't exist. I let it (the fear) go!

Let's continue on the subject of screen time for a moment. As a parent, I realized I had a lot of preconceived fears, thoughts and worries about screen time. None of them were based in any personal experience or were backed up by any research.

I started to experiment as the kids got older and as we started living through three months, then six, and then nine months of a global pandemic. I wanted to see what would happen in our house if I didn't worry so much about it. Spoiler alert: not so much. I realized by being observant that I would always know when it became a problem, and I had the tools to collaboratively fix it with my kids' help and my husband's input.

Reminder: quality matters just as much as quantity.

I let my kids watch other people play video games on YouTube. No, I don't get it. I have no idea why they want to do that. Yes, I secretly wish my kids could make 11 million dollars a year, like Ryan of *Ryan's Toy Review* and financially support us, but now I'm off topic.

I have a few rules, which have remained consistent. Sometimes, I get a feeling that it's been enough. I give my kids a 15-to-30-minute warning and all the tech goes off for an hour or two. YouTube is not allowed after dinner. After dinner tech consists of sibling or family time playing video games or enjoying a sporting event, movie or show together.

There are some exceptions because we must parent different kids differently. For example, if Gabi comes home from dance and gets right in the shower, she is allowed twenty minutes of any tech she wants while she eats her second dinner. She needs this to decompress from all the sensory stimulation and she eats better this way, too. Win, Win!

Does this follow the AAP guidelines for screen time limits? Yikes! I don't even know. Because I let that go, too, and stopped looking it up! Learning to do this has been freeing and I cannot wait for you to allow yourself to do the same.

Key Points for Busy Moms and Dads

Ask yourself a few questions before a power struggle begins:

1. "Can I let this go?
2. What will happen if I do?
3. If I don't?"

Conclusion

Conclusion

It's been more than a year since Covid-19 entered our lives. As a behavioral specialist, both professionally and personally, I've used some of this time to reflect on my parenting journey. From all of the impressive books I have read, through all the excellent training I have received, and considering all the trial and error I've experienced with my own kids, I have found that the single most important element of my parenting is the ability to empathize and validate.

In the first few days of the pandemic, when our life came to a grinding halt, my kids were much more upset about cancelled games, activities, play dates and vacations than the rising death toll of Covid-19. I reminded myself that their reaction was to be expected, that it really wasn't surprising for children to see the world through the lens of their own needs and desires. Why should a pandemic, something they largely could not comprehend (who could?) cause them to redefine the parameters of their daily existence? They were feeling what they *should* have been feeling.

With that in mind, I right sized my expectations and showed them *soooo* much empathy. This wasn't easy because I was scared and angry at the world, and I still am. However, I made empathy my mantra and I kept at it each and every day. Within a week, my kids stopped yelling at me and giving me sass whenever they could. They started showing empathy toward each other and it's still happening!

Ruby has become my ally, my home-learning assistant, and the third adult in the house—that is until she has her moments of absolutely falling apart when she remembers all that she has lost. But instead of expressing her pain by yelling at everyone in her path, she cries and talks to me about her feelings. I even encouraged her to write, to vent and let it out, and she's on her way to becoming a new blog contributor.

I'm getting to know my kids again on an intense level I hadn't imagined. They haven't been home like this since they were infants and toddlers, and even then they had preschool, babysitters, and grandparents to share the load. We made it well through the end of the 2019-2020 school year. When school started remotely in the fall, I was there all over to support the children as their empathy coordinator.

I had to agree with them: the situation sucked, and it wasn't fair. Our only consolation was remembering that we weren't the only family living under these conditions. But we were the only family living in our house!

Three weeks later, when school returned to in-person classes for half-days, the children were scared of how it would go and I was just as concerned as they were, if not more. When it only took four weeks before school went back to full remote, I empathized with my three students because this time it sucked even more and felt beyond unfair.

I made sure to give the empathy stage a lot of time. Then, and only then, did I slowly point out the positives and the silver linings of being home as we were: PJs all day, more sleep, school in the basement on our swings, on beanbags, at our new desks, on the couch, in a quiet space and next to mom...all the perks of at-home learning, which we enjoyed, but I still allowed and empathized with the sadness and frustration my kids were feeling.

With no books out yet about parenting through a pandemic, I continued to do things that made all of us happy, like having whipped cream in the house for no reason at all and buying Halloween bags of bite-sized candy months before Halloween. Hopefully, I haven't set any precedents that we can't undo later. In fact, even though this has been a strange time, in some ways, I think we'll be forever changed for the better.

Maybe whipped cream is better for us than the ingredients suggest...

I feel as if I'm writing a parenting book during a time when parenting has reached a sort of epic status. I should take a stab at a gnawing question, which lurks in the back of the mind of all parents: *How do I know if I'm a good parent?*

Good parents do not have to follow all my advice—nor anyone else's, for that matter.

Good parents fail all the time, nonstop.

Good parents also succeed.

We stink up the joint. Sometimes we do it well and sometimes we don't. In fact, sometimes we're super ungraceful. But good parents pick themselves up, reflect, and try a different approach. We all strive to be good, but the *best* parents are the ones that keep trying.

If your new strategy of "the more whipped cream the better" turns into a stomachache for your 11-year-old, use it as a teachable moment and move on. I know I did. If you're failing often, which is a relative statistic—and I don't recommend keeping score—it's because you're awesome and striving to make things better. It's true, and if you're not sure if this applies to you, just ask for and make sure you get some validation.

Like many self-made people, I've had major imposter syndrome running my company, writing this book, and working with parents. How can I give advice when I just yelled at my kids over a cold bowl of macaroni and cheese? That's when I remember that the perfect parent doesn't exist. Humans make mistakes.

The question is, what you do with those moments? Do you go back and apologize to your kids? Do you think about why you lost it over another instant dinner? Do you have your children take some responsibility for Mommy losing her temper? Yep, I do. I apologize for the way I handled whatever it is I botched, and we talk about why it happened and how to do better next time. We acknowledge that it takes two (or sometimes five in my house) to tango, but the important thing is, we keep dancing!

So meanwhile, keep reading; keep listening; keep questioning and keep trying. Oh yeah, keep laughing, too.

I know you're a great parent because if you're reading this … you must be!

Resources

Resources

"Help! I need a childhood expert!"

"Somebody must know more than I do!"

"Where's that Resources section when I need it?"

Sound familiar? We've got you covered, whether it's an expert or a specialist or just someone who knows a little bit more and can help, you're in the right place.

When Should I Get My Child Professional Help?

Depending on the age of your kids and a host of other variables, that moment could come at any time. Here are some for you to consider:

1. A teacher or other school, camp, or recreation professional, has recommended it. Sometimes, these adults spend more time with our kids than we do, and they work with hundreds, if not thousands of kids a year, so I would take their suggestion very seriously.

2. My child's low moods, anxious thoughts or behavior has become disruptive to their lives and/or our family's during most days of the week.

3. My child is making statements, such as, "I'm bad" or "No one loves me" or "No one Likes me." Negative self-assessments like this, and those showing low self-esteem, should be red flags.

4. You feel like you need help as a parent! It's good to admit that. No one needs to be a hero here. It's never a bad idea to get outside support!

Psychologists, Social Workers, Licensed Professional Counselors

These are three types of mental health counselors you may come across if you are looking for a therapist for your child. Psychologists receive the most schooling, however that doesn't necessarily mean they will be the best fit for your child. Check out their websites, see what types of mental health they specialize in and what type of therapeutic approach they use. If your child is younger than 13 or 14, you will meet with the therapist first as parents and periodically while they are receiving individual therapy. If you have a young child and are in need of support, look for a therapist that is comfortable with play-based therapy. Even tweens benefit from this approach. In looking for the "right fit" therapist, ask your local mom groups, your school social worker and/or your pediatrician and then set up a few phone calls so you can get a feel for the right fit. Though it may be time consuming and costly, be prepared, as it often takes a few tries to find the right fit for your child.

Coaches

First, look for someone with real credentials. Coaching is a relatively new field. There are many types of coaching certifications, however, I prefer to look at the background of each individual coach. If you are looking for a business coach, you want someone who has been successful in business and/or working with employees. Similarly, if you consider using a coach for your child, make sure they have significant experience working with kids like yours. Teachers, special educators, and mental health professionals all have great experience and may be helpful if your children are struggling with behavior, routine, executive functioning, study skills or academics.

BCBA (Board Certified Behavior Analyst)

They are trained to supervise ABA therapies for those with Autism or related conditions.

ABA TECH

They are trained to work under a BCBA and actually do the ABA therapy sessions. For more about ABA Therapy, visit childmind.org

Occupational Therapists (OT)

They may be helpful if you have a sensory sensitive child. This could include extremely picky eating, extreme difficulty with clothing (maybe only wearing one or two pieces of clothing without complaint), noise sensitivity, being unable to handle textures and messiness, such as finger painting, crafts, sand, etc. An OT can also be helpful with kids who are clumsy and seem out of balance or have trouble sitting up. An OT can also work on fine motor skills, such as, handwriting, feeding, buttons and zippers.

Physical Therapists

According to the American Physical Therapist Association, "Physical therapists (PTs) are movement experts who optimize quality of life through prescribed exercise, hands-on care, and patient education.

Physical therapists teach patients how to prevent or manage their condition so that they will achieve long-term health benefits. PTs examine each individual and develop a plan, using treatment techniques to promote the ability to move, reduce pain, restore function, and prevent disability. In addition, PTs work with individuals to prevent the loss of mobility before it occurs by developing fitness- and wellness-oriented programs for healthier and more active lifestyles."

For more information visit, APTA.org.

Psychiatrists and Nurse Practitioners

These professionals work with therapists to prescribe medication for mental health and certain neurological disabilities, such as ADHD.

Miscellaneous

The Centers for Disease Control (CDC)
A guide for children from birth to five years old.
(cdc.gov/ncbddd/actearly/milestones/index.html)

The American Academy of Pediatrics
A parent and caregiver site for children five years and older.
(healthychildren.org/english/ages-stages/pages/default.aspx)

Faab Consulting

Welcome to the home of Franki Bagdade consulting:
www.faabconsulting.com

About the Author

About the Author

Franki Bagdade graduated from Michigan State University with a BA in Elementary Education. She received her MA in Special Education from Wayne State University. She is currently enjoying her largest "pandemic purchase" and is half-way through earning her master's in clinical social work at University of Kentucky.

She has spent more than 20 years specializing in the world of children with extra needs, including non-traditional learning environments, camp settings, and everything in between.

Her traditional mainstream educational experience includes all types of general classroom teaching, running a special needs resource room, consulting for pre-school through high school resource programs, and conducting training sessions for professional development. Most recently, she was the assistant director of Tamarack Camps, one of the largest overnight camps in North America.

Franki is the owner and founder of FAAB Consulting, which offers academic and behavioral guidance for schools and camps and behavioral coaching for families.

Please visit our website, read our blog, and follow us on Facebook and Instagram.

Franki lives with her husband, Jeff, and her three notorious children in West Bloomfield, Michigan.

A portion of the proceeds from sales
of this book will be donated to Friendship Circle of Michigan.

Other MSI Press Publications on Parenting

10 Quick Homework Tips (McKinley Alder & Trombly)

108 Yoga and Self-Care Practices for Busy Mamas (Gentile)

365 Teacher Secrets for Parents: Fun Ways to Help Your Child in Elementary School (McKinley Alder & Trombly)

Choice and Structure for Children with Autism (McNeil)

Clean Your Plate! 13 Things Good Parents Say That Ruin Kids' Lives (Bayardelle)

Girl, You Got This! A Fitness Trainer's Personal Strategies for Success Transitioning into Motherhood (Renz)

How to Be a Good Mommy When You're Sick: A Guide to Motherhood with Chronic Illness (Graves)

Lamentations of the Heart Mingles with Peace and Joy (Wells-Smith)

Lessons of Labor: One Woman's Self-Discovery through Birth and Motherhood (Aziz)

Life after Losing a Child (Romer & Young)

Mommy Poisoned Our House Guest (Shenan Leaver)

Noah's New Puppy (Rice & Henderson)

One Simple Text...The Liz Marks Story (Shaw & Brown)

Parenting in a Pandemic (Bayardelle)

Soccer Is Fun without Parents (Jonas)

Understanding the Challenge of "No" for Children with Autism (McNeil)

I *Love* My Kids, But I Don't Always *Like* Them